ALAN RICHARDSON

The Bible in the Age of Science

The Cadbury Lectures
in the
University of Birmingham
1961

SCM PRESS LTD
BLOOMSBURY STREET LONDON

© SCM PRESS LTD 1961
FIRST PUBLISHED 1961
SECOND IMPRESSION 1964
PRINTED IN HOLLAND BY
DRUKKERIJ HOLLAND N.V. AMSTERDAM

SCM PAPERBACKS

now published

MEN OF UNITY *by Stephen Neill*

THE MIND OF JESUS *by William Barclay*

CRUCIFIED AND CROWNED *by William Barclay*

JESUS AS THEY SAW HIM *by William Barclay*

EPILOGUES AND PRAYERS *by William Barclay*

NEW TESTAMENT WORDS *by William Barclay*

ST PAUL AND THE GOSPEL OF JESUS
by Charles E. Raven

THE BIBLE IN THE AGE OF SCIENCE *by Alan Richardson*

INTRODUCING THE CHRISTIAN FAITH *by A. M. Ramsey,
Archbishop of Canterbury*

THE BRITISH CHURCHES TODAY *by Kenneth Slack*

CHRISTIAN DEVIATIONS: THE CHALLENGE OF THE SECTS
by Horton Davies

DESPATCH FROM NEW DELHI *by Kenneth Slack*

NEW DELHI SPEAKS: *World Council of Churches*

LOOKING AT THE VATICAN COUNCIL *by Bernard Pawley*

BEGINNING THE OLD TESTAMENT *by Erik Routley*

GOD'S CROSS IN OUR WORLD *by David L. Edwards*

CHRISTIAN FAITH AND LIFE *by William Temple*

WE THE PEOPLE *by Kathleen Bliss*

HONEST TO GOD *by John A. T. Robinson*

THE HONEST TO GOD DEBATE *edited by David L. Edwards*

PHILOSOPHERS AND RELIGIOUS TRUTH *by Ninian Smart*

A TIME FOR UNITY *by Oliver Tomkins*

CONTENTS

Preface   7

1   The Scientific Revolution   9

2   The Revolution in Historical Thinking   32

3   The Revolution in Theological Thinking   54

4   From Schleiermacher to Barth   77

5   The Existentialist Theology   100

6   The *Heilsgeschichte* Theology   122

7   The Theology of Images   142

8   The Fulfilment of the Scriptures   164

    Index of Names   187

    Index of Subjects   190

THE COVER

The illustration is of the radio telescope at
Jodrell Bank, Cheshire.

PREFACE

WHEN the Council and Senate of the University of Birmingham invited me to deliver the Edward Cadbury Lectures in the Spring Term of 1961, I was deeply conscious both of the honour of the invitation and also of the responsibility which it entailed. I was well aware of the high estimation in which the Lectureship stands not only by reason of the notable benefactor of learning whose name it bears but also because of the distinction of its former lecturers. I nevertheless determined to accept the opportunity thus offered to set in order my reflections upon a theme which must constantly be present to the mind of a theologian whose own teaching work is carried out in the context of life in a modern University. It seemed to me that a consideration of the ancient biblical revelation in the light of the scientific and historical advances of the modern period might fittingly be undertaken under the auspices of the University of Birmingham, where theological studies and scientific investigations are alike pursued with academic distinction in quest of that ultimate unity of truth which the very existence of *uni*versities attests. Whatever may be the successes or failures of the enterprise here attempted, I desire to express my gratitude to the Council and Senate of the University for the opportunity thus given and for the kindness and consideration which have been extended to me during the delivering of these Edward Cadbury Lectures.

While I was engaged upon their preparation, I received two other invitations which I felt it to be both my privilege and my duty to accept. I was asked by the Faculty of Theology in the University of Otago, New Zealand, to deliver the Thomas Burns Memorial Lectures in July, 1960. This book contains the substance of the lectures which I delivered in Knox Theological Hall in Dunedin, and I am glad to take this opportunity of acknowledging my respect for the scholars of the Otago Theological Faculty and of expressing my gratitude for the welcome and friendship which I experienced in Dunedin; in particular I wish to record my thanks to my kind hosts, Professor John Henderson and the Bishop of Dunedin. The second invitation came from the Senatus of the Theological Hall, Ormond College, Melbourne, Victoria, where in August, 1960 I delivered the Alexander Love Memorial Lectures upon the themes of several of the chapters in this book. To my host, the Rev. Professor J. Davis McCaughey, Master of Ormond College, I would especially desire to record my appreciation and thanks. To other friends, new and old, in New Zealand and Australia, I am happy to acknowledge my indebtedness for many things, not least for participation in ecumenical fellowship of the kind which is stimulating, enriching and enduring.

ALAN RICHARDSON

1

THE SCIENTIFIC REVOLUTION

THE age of science is the period which succeeded the disintegration of the mediaeval world-view in the sixteenth century. It may be said to have dawned with the publication of a treatise by the Polish churchman Copernicus, *De Revolutionibus Orbium Coelestium,* in 1543, the year of its author's death. In this work Copernicus, not desirous of challenging the established geocentric view of immemorial tradition, put forward as a merely tentative hypothesis the suggestion that the earth goes round the sun; as a mathematical exercise he shewed that such an hypothesis was a good deal simpler than the increasingly elaborate theories about cycles and epicycles which were needed to account for the observable motions of the heavenly orbs on the basis of the old geocentric hypothesis. There the matter might have rested, as an interesting exercise in mathematics, had it not been for the development in the years after Copernicus' death of what we know as the experimental method in science. The experimental method consists simply in devising experiments by means of which hypotheses may be tested. Stated in this way, it seems to us such an obvious procedure as hardly to deserve mentioning. But we live in a scientific age, and we find it difficult to remember that its ways of thinking are barely yet four hundred years old. Down to the close of the Middle Ages, however, questions of fact were settled not by experiment but by authority. Broadly speaking, authority in spiritual matters was represented by the Bible, while authority in what we would call scientific questions was represented by Aristotle. Aristotle had in fact considered the hypothesis that the earth is not the centre of the universe, which had been put forward by the Pythagoreans; but he had rejected it. The retrograde Aristotelian view[1] that the earth is the centre of the universe, and that the stars are animate beings set in a series of concentric crystal spheres surrounding it, was developed into an impressive cosmological system by Ptolemy of Alexandria (A.D. 90-168), who gathered up in his great treatise, the *Almagest,* practically all the astronomical knowledge and speculation of the ancient world. The 'Ptolemaic system' was accepted by the Byzantine East and was introduced into the Latin West by the Arabs; hence the Arabic title by which his treatise is known. It dominated the minds of educated men until long after the death of Copernicus; it described the universe not only of Dante but of Shakespeare.

The influence of Aristotle prevailed during the later Middle Ages not only in cosmology but throughout the whole range of 'natural philosophy' and 'natural (i.e. philosophical) theology'. Again it was the Arabs who were initially responsible for this somewhat surprising state of affairs, in which a pagan thinker who had been dead for well over a millennium had come to dominate the thought of Christendom at the zenith of its mediaeval development. Arabic scholars had fashioned out of the rediscovered works of Aristotle a pantheistic philosophy which made the traditional Augustinian Platonism of Christian theologians seem antiquated and untenable. Ideas are not dangerous until they are backed by physical power; but now the vast military and economic

[1] Cf. A. E. Taylor, *Aristotle,* London and Edinburgh, 1919, 79: 'What Aristotle did, and it is perhaps the most retrograde step ever taken in the history of a science, was ... to introduce into physics the disastrous theory, which it was a great part of Galileo's life-work to destroy, that the stuff of which the spheres are made is a "fifth body", different from the (four) "elements" of which the bodies among which we live are made.'

power of Islam half encircled the small world of Christendom, compressing it in a pincer-hold from the Balkans round by Sicily and North Africa to Spain. The threat from the new materialistic philosophy, backed by such immense material force, may be compared with the challenge of Marxism to the Christian lands of eastern Europe after the October Revolution in 1917. The new Aristotelian logic, employed by the Arabian philosophers as the instrument of their atheistic doctrines, was infiltrating into the universities of Christendom and making a strong appeal to the younger generation and to the intelligentsia of the rising mercantile classes. It was then that St Thomas Aquinas (1225-74), following in the direction pointed out by his teacher, Albertus Magnus, performed his supreme feat of Christian apologetics: he took the new Aristotelian logic and turned it into an instrument for the defence of Christian truth. His *Summa Contra Gentiles* is perhaps the most remarkable and the most successful Christian apology ever written. Like every true apologist, St Thomas takes the new thinking of his day and turns it into a weapon for the defence of Christian truth. Though condemned during his lifetime even by members of his own Dominican order, his arguments were soon triumphant throughout Christendom, and he became 'the Angelic Doctor'. Aristotle, now rescued from servitude to Averroistic materialism, became the authority whose pronouncements determined every question of natural philosophy.

So well had Aquinas succeeded in Christianizing Aristotle that when the authority of Aristotle in the sphere of astronomy or physics was called in question, it seemed as though Christian truth itself was being impiously assailed. So completely had Aristotle and the Bible been harmonized in the mediaeval synthesis of natural and revealed theology that the overthrow of Aristotelian philosophy by the rise of modern science seemed to the Aristotelian philosophers, though not to the new scientists themselves, to involve the rejection of the biblical revelation as well. The one indubitable truth which we learn from a study of the history of philosophy is that of the impermanence of philosophical points of view. The brave new logic of yesterday becomes the stuffy orthodoxy of today and the deadly obscurantism of tomorrow. Between the thirteenth and sixteenth centuries the revived Aristotelianism had passed through all these stages. The world-view which the new scientific movement had to destroy before it could come to maturity was that based on Aristotle and Ptolemy; it was not derived from the Bible, and, in the event, the Bible has continued to exercise authority over the minds of men long after Aristotle has been deposed. But this is because the rise of modern science has gradually helped us to see more clearly that what is revealed in the Bible is not a cosmology or any kind of truth which can be investigated or verified by scientific method. Those who in the sixteenth century could not dissociate their thinking from the old Aristotelian notions inevitably tended to believe that the new science was subversive of truth as such, including the revealed truth of the Bible; but the men of science themselves did not believe this, and the passage of time has shewn that they were right. Copernicus' fancy, that the mathematics of astronomy would be greatly simplified if one assumed that the earth rotated daily on its axis, instead of assuming that the whole heavens revolved at an incredible speed every twenty-four hours, would have remained a theme of academic conversation if the authority of Aristotle had not been swept aside. In the event, however, the name of Copernicus became attached to the first triumphant revolution achieved by the new experimental method of modern science, although it was not Copernicus who devised the means by which his novel speculation could be verified.

The Ptolemaic system, which had for centuries seemed so simple and natural, slowly appeared to be increasingly complicated and artificial as observations of the heavenly bodies became more accurate. Then came discoveries like those of the Danish astronomer Tycho Brahe (1546-1601), which refuted the time-honoured view of Aristotle that the regions beyond the moon were incorruptible, changeless and perfect; in 1572 he had found a brilliant new star in the constellation Cassiopeia far beyond the distance of the moon, and he calculated that the comet of 1577 was twice as far again as the moon was from the earth. But beyond all such considerations there was coming to birth in the opening decades of the seventeenth century a new way of looking at things, which took its stand upon observation and induction rather than upon authority and tradition. Its new concept of mechanism was completely irreconcilable with the old pre-scientific Aristotelian mythology of nature. The Aristotelian universe was controlled by intelligences which rolled the spheres with their affixed planets in rational patterns; natural objects had dispositions or even souls which moved them to go from one place to another; the increasing velocity of a falling body indicated its pleasure in moving towards its natural home at the centre of the universe; values, purposes and desires were thus regarded as categories of scientific explanation. The new mechanistic way of looking at things was making it more and more difficult to regard Aristotle's 'Physics' as science at all. It was not simply that new facts were being seen but that old facts were being seen in a new perspective. Aristotle himself had been a close and astute observer of natural phenomena, and the later mediaevals knew much more about mechanics than is generally recognized.[1] It is true that the object of the mediaeval investigators was to amend the Aristotelian system at its weakest points, but the refutation of that system was implicit in their work. Whether we choose to apply the word 'science' to their activities depends upon how we define the word; but the recent study of the history of mediaeval thought

[1] See Marshall Clagett, *The Science of Mechanics in the Middle Ages,* Madison: University of Wisconsin Press, 1959.

tends to shew that there is more justification for speaking of mediaeval science than for the widespread but uncritical use of the expression 'Greek science'.

If we use 'science' in its ancient sense of knowledge in general (*scientia*), then, of course, we must speak of Greek science—and of Egyptian science and Babylonian science and mediaeval science. Or again, if we are speaking of mathematical science, then the Greeks knew a great deal about it, especially geometry. Every schoolboy knows the name of Euclid (c. 300 B.C.), the Alexandrian scholar who gathered together in his *Elements* all the mathematical knowledge which had accumulated since the days of Pythagoras in the sixth century B.C. But mathematics is a deductive, not an empirical, science; it deduces truths from ideal concepts such as triangles, circles, numbers and symbols. It is science which can be worked out (in principle, even if not by us non-mathematicians!) in an arm-chair with one's eyes closed; it does not involve the actual observation of nature, and its truths would be true if the natural order were to disappear overnight. The Greek view of knowledge regarded mathematical knowledge as the true type and ideal of knowledge as such; Plato conceived of reality itself as consisting of pure Ideas which were knowable not by the senses but only by *theoria,* intellectual contemplation. Aristotle, it is true, thought that the content of the Ideas must be known through observation, and he was, as we have said, a shrewd and careful observer of nature. But for him also, as for the Greeks in general, mathematics was the true science, and the observation of nature (as in astronomy, of which the Greeks, Babylonians and Egyptians knew a good deal) was primarily a matter of searching for pure mathematical forms in the natural order. If one is convinced that the pure rational form is the circle and that nature is ordered by rational intelligences, then one will tend to regard any appearance of elliptical movement in nature as an error of human observation, since we tend to see only what we are convinced *must* be there; we look for evidence which will confirm our *a priori* conceptions and we simply do not see things which do not conform to them. The Greeks never discovered the empirical method in science primarily because they were not looking at things from an empirical point of view. Archimedes (287-212 B.C.), the mathematician who discovered the value of π, conducted experiments with levers, being something of a practical engineer, but he never discovered the experimental method. Greek architects certainly knew how to apply mathematical knowledge to the work in hand, but this is still not what we mean by modern scientific method. The chief reason why the Greeks never developed natural science in the modern sense was that they thought of knowledge (on the analogy of geometry) as something that is deduced from first principles, not something that can be acquired from the observation of nature by the method of induction and experiment. But other reasons are also to hand. Supporters of the economic interpretation of history would point out that natural science could not flourish under an economy in which all manual work must be performed by slaves: Aristotle's gentleman-philosopher could not become a scientist because he would not get his hands dirty. We need not be Marxists to recognize that there is an element of truth in the notion that certain economic arrangements in society are less, and some more, congenial to the development of the scientific attitude. To this day it is the classical element in the western cultural tradition, not the Hebraic-Christian, which affects to despise technology; in the biblical view of life it is not considered undignified to work in a carpenter's shop or *(a posteriori)* in a laboratory. Still another reason why science in the modern sense was not developed by the Greeks was their lack of an adequate numerical notation; advanced arithmetic is hardly possible when numbers have to be written by means of all the letters of the alphabet and the significance of the number ten is unrecognized. (Anyone who doubts this should try writing down a column of figures in Roman numerals, say XLIV, XCVIII, IX and CXI, and then trying to add them up.) Modern science would not have gone very far if Arabic civilization in the Middle Ages had not developed the system of decimal numeration which was probably learnt originally from Indian mathematicians.[1] For all these reasons, and doubtless others too, the Greeks were a long way from conceiving of anything in the nature of empirical science as it has developed since the sixteenth century of the Christian era, and if we use the expression 'Greek science' at all, we must not be misled into thinking that it was something of the same order as our modern science; it was in reality thinking with different presuppositions and different aims. Modern science, that skilful commingling of mathematics with observation, hypothesis and controlled experiment, did not grow out of Greek science as a mature plant grows from a seed; the contributions both of Arabic and of Christian civilization had to be made before modern science could be born. It is hardly an exaggeration to say that the only contribution made by the Greeks, apart from their geometry, to the natural sciences was their names. In point of fact, modern empirical science could not set out upon its course before the European mind had been liberated from the toils of Greek pseudo-science.

The struggle of the new scientists against the old order was not a struggle of 'science' against 'religion' but the revolt of the new scientific philosophy against the old Aristotelian pseudo-scientific philosophy. The people who attempted to use the might of the Inquisition to silence Galileo were the conservative Aristotelian philosophers, who realized with horror that the novel doctrines of Copernicus, if they were

---

[1] The very name of that generalized arithmetic known as Algebra is derived from the first word of the title of a work by the Arabian mathematician, Alkarismi, a contemporary of Charlemagne.

allowed to be propagated, would undermine their own authority as arbiters of orthodoxy by proving false what they had taught to be true. The real issue, of course, was not the truth of the Bible but the truth of Aristotle and the authority of the Aristotelian theologians themselves. Galileo's 'crime' was that he challenged the security of officialdom; his teaching was an attack upon 'the establishment'. Galileo's trial before the Inquisition is often represented as a decisive moment in the history of freedom of thought. Men still become highly emotional over the picture of the brave martyr in the cause of science who withstood the cruel and arrogant dogmatism of ignorant churchmen. Actually the blacks and whites were much more confused, the issues more complicated and the motives on each side more mixed than they appear in the popular picture.[1] It is hardly necessary at this

---

[1] After having been censured in 1616 because of his Copernican views and having promised to teach them no more, Galileo nevertheless published in 1632 a refutation of the Aristotelian cosmology. It took the form of a Dialogue in which the participants were a Copernican, a Ptolemaic astronomer and a stupid Aristotelian philosopher. Personalities became involved, and it was represented to the Pope, Urban VIII (formerly Galileo's old friend, Cardinal Barberini), that the Aristotelian was a caricature of himself. The Inquisition forced Galileo, now an old man of seventy, to recant on his knees and condemned him to imprisonment. The legend that after recanting his view that the earth is in motion he murmured under his breath *E pur si muove* ('But it does move') is generally admitted to be apocryphal; its earliest appearance was in 1761. Pope Urban remitted the sentence of imprisonment and Galileo lived on, blind and deaf, but still bitterly satirical against the Aristotelians to the end, until his death at the (for those days) advanced age of seventy-eight in 1642. There is no evidence that he was ever tortured. See G. de Santillana, *The Crime of Galileo*, London, 1958, for the most recent account; the same writer contributed an introduction to Galileo's *Dialogue on the Great World Systems* (The Salusbury translation), Chicago, 1953. Albert Einstein contributed a foreword to the translation by Stillman Drake, *Dialogue concerning the Two Chief World Systems — Ptolemaic and Copernican*, University of California Press, Los Angeles, 1953. See also *The Private Life of Galileo*

date to labour the point that Galileo's controversy was not
with the biblical revelation but with the Aristotelian natural
philosophy. The Rationalist Myth, which grew up in the
nineteenth century, is now discredited, though it still lives
on in certain popular histories of science. According to this
myth the Greeks of the classical age had laid the foundations
both of science and of intellectual freedom, but the onward
march of mankind towards the twin goals of scientific truth
and intellectual liberty had been interrupted by the long
night of theological dogmatism and ecclesiastical authoritar-
ianism which had supervened upon the conversion of the
Emperor Constantine in the fourth century A.D. As the pagan
Emperor, Julian the Apostate (A.D. 332-363), at the beginning of the 'night', and the poet of the new age of progress
at the end of it had both lamented, the 'pale Galilean' had
conquered and the world had grown grey from his breath.[1]
According to the Rationalist Myth, the men of science at
the Renaissance, with the rekindled lights of Hellas shining
on their faces, courageously withstood the entrenched
arrogance of ecclesiastical dogmatism, and, amidst the
fanatical religious wars and persecutions of the sixteenth and
seventeenth centuries, began the great assault upon the
tyranny of religion and ignorance. But, as we have noted,
Greek science was not the inspiration of the modern scientific
movement; it had to be demolished and a new start had to
be made before modern science could begin. The Myth does
less than justice to Galileo and his fellow pioneers, because
it minimizes the magnitude of their achievement. They were
not in fact taking up a quest which the ancient Greeks had
been forced to lay down; they were starting an entirely new
venture of the human spirit.

compiled principally from his correspondence and that of his
eldest daughter, Sister Maria Celeste, London (Macmillan and
Co.), 1870.
[1] A. C. Swinburne (1837-1909), *Hymn to Proserpine*.

Furthermore, it is a simple mistake to regard the conflicts of Galileo with the Aristotelians as typical of the relations of the new scientists with religious authority in Europe generally. In England, for instance, there was no conflict between 'science' and 'religion', no struggle for freedom of enquiry against ecclesiastical or political authority, no persecution of the new experimenters. The great scientific revolution took place quietly and without fuss. The new thought enjoyed high patronage both in Church and State. The Lord Keeper of the Great Seal to Queen Elizabeth I (Francis Bacon, Baron Verulam of Verulam, 1561-1626) had appointed himself a kind of public relations officer of the new scientific movement and wrote his famous treatise, *Novum Organum* (1620), in praise of induction as the great new instrument of man's control over nature. In 1662 the religious and social approbation of the whole scientific enterprise was attested by the incorporation of the Royal Society under a charter from King Charles II. The greatest figure in seventeenth century science, Isaac Newton, whose *Principia Mathematica* (1687) gathered into an all-embracing system the achievements of the scientific movement since the days of Copernicus, was rewarded with appointment as Master of the Mint (1699) and was knighted by Queen Anne. The old Aristotelian philosophy had passed away peacefully and the new mechanistic cosmology had been duly installed as its successor. The notion that the biblical revelation had been impugned in any way had not occurred to anyone, least of all to Newton himself, who spent long hours with the Bible trying to solve with its aid the problems of world-chronology. Indeed, it was generally agreed that Newton's demonstration that all the movements of bodies in space, whether falling apples or the revolutions of the heavenly orbs, could be described by a single law, was a signal vindication of the teleological argument (the 'argument from design') for the existence of God; the *Principia Mathematica* was a kind of

scientific commentary upon Psalm 19, 'The heavens declare
the glory of God, and the firmament sheweth his handy-
work'. What the Psalmist had understood by revelation
Newton had demonstrated by reason and experiment.[1]
Christian apologists of the eighteenth century did not find it
necessary to defend the faith against the new science. The
most famous of them, Bishop Joseph Butler, whose *Analogy
of Religion* was published in 1736, hardly refers at all to the
new cosmology, though he clearly thinks of it as corrobor-
ating the truth of Natural Religion; in one place he says that
our notions of the plan of Providence need to be enlarged in
a manner 'proportionable to what late discoveries have enlarged our views with respect to the material world,' and he
adds, 'It is certain that, as the material world appears to be,
in a manner, boundless and immense, there must be some
scheme of Providence in proportion to it.'[2]

There were indeed inevitably many conflicts in the age
which witnessed the birth of modern science, but they did
not fall into a pattern of 'science' versus 'religion'. The most
far-reaching revolution in men's understanding of nature
that had ever taken place was being accomplished, and it is
natural that at such a time there should be widespread uncertainty and confusion about the issues at stake, even in
those countries like England in which the great reorientation

---

[1] So Joseph Addison (1672-1719) re-writes the Psalm in the spirit
of the new scientific philosophy; the 'radiant orbs' of Newton's
clean and empty heavens were the apostles in every land of the
works of an Almighty Hand:

> In reason's ear they all rejoice,
> And utter forth a glorious voice,
> For ever singing as they shine,
> 'The hand that made us is divine.'

The Spacious Firmament on High.

[2] *The Analogy of Religion,* Butler's Works, Oxford, Clarendon
Press, 1874, Vol. I, 67f.

was unopposed by authority.[1] Mediaeval and modern existed together in strange proximity; the two worlds, if we may borrow phrases from a later age, dwelt in peaceful co-existence, or, what comes to the same thing, in a state of cold war. Important new facts about the universe were coming to light every year; every year scores of old women were being burnt at the stake as witches. Religious fanaticism and enthusiasm for scientific experiment were alike characteristic of the times. The new scientific ideas and attitudes cut right across confessional loyalties as they cut across the frontiers of nationality. Catholic disagreed with Catholic and Protestant with Protestant about the value of the new methods and theories. Luther and Melanchthon disapproved of the heliocentric speculations and were typically mediaeval in their attitude towards the new scientific ways of thinking, while at the same time they were vigorously attacking the Aristotelian theology of the Schoolmen; and it was a Lutheran theologian, Osiander, who advocated the publication of the Catholic Copernicus' *De Revolutionibus Orbium,* arranged for its publication, wrote a preface to it, and presented a copy of it to its timid author upon his death-bed. The Protestant Theological Faculty at Tübingen ought to have noticed that the Bible, which declared emphatically that the heavens would pass away like an outworn garment (Ps. 102.26; Heb. 1.11f.), was at variance with the Aristotelian doctrine of the eternity, immutability and perfection of the planetary spheres; but it persecuted the Protestant Johannes Kepler (1571-1630) whose discoveries refuted the Ptolemaic cosmology and paved the way for Newton's brilliant synthesis. Fleeing for safety from Protestant to Catholic, from Catholic to Protestant, poor Kepler, in permanent ill-health and poverty, was forced to practise astrology in order to make a living; the man to whom the great Tycho Brahe had

[1] A fascinating presentation of the English scene at this period will be found in Rose Macaulay's fine novel, *They Were Defeated.*

bequeathed his astronomical notes and who developed
Tycho's researches into his famous three laws which govern
the motions of the planets had to look on while his own
mother stood trial for witchcraft during the hysteria which
swept through Europe in the second decade of the seventeenth century.[1] In Kepler's life and misfortunes the agon-
izing clash of mediaeval and modern is seen in microcosm.

Kepler was a man of deep religious conviction, and in this
respect also he is truly representative of the whole scientific
movement of the seventeenth century and beyond it.
Amongst the forces which gave rise to modern science there
was clearly a powerful religious impetus. Kepler himself
propounded the mechanistic hypothesis as the expression of
his almost mystical assurance that the glory of God was dis-
played in the clockwork perfection of the material universe.[2]
The French philosopher of the new scientific approach,
René Descartes (1596-1650), who in his small but influential *Discours de la Méthode* (1637) proposed the method
of universal doubt in its most stringent form, did so in order
to rid himself of the last vestiges of scholastic Aristotelian
dogmatism; he reintroduced into his philosophy the 'ontological argument' for the existence of God, which Aquinas
and the Aristotelians had abandoned, and he made God the
ground of certitude in philosophical thinking. Blaise Pascal
(1623-62), whose mathematical genius opened the way to
the differential calculus, expressed a deep awareness of the
personal or existential element in the knowledge of God, the
God of the Bible, the God of Abraham, Isaac and Jacob, not
the God of the schoolmen, the Unmoved Mover of the
Aristotelian philosophy.[3] He renewed the older Augustinian

[1] See the fine study by Max Caspar, *Kepler,* Eng. trans. by C. Doris
    Hellmann, London (Abelard-Schuman), 1959.
[2] See Herbert Butterfield, *The Origins of Modern Science, 1300-
    1800,* London, 1950, 59 and 105.
[3] Amongst the many studies of Pascal attention may be drawn to
    one of the most recent, Ernest Mortimer's *Blaise Pascal: the Life*

affirmation that the universal quest of man in search of God is itself evidence that man has, however dimly, already apprehended God, or rather been apprehended by him. Robert Boyle (1627-91), one of the founders and first Fellows of the Royal Society, the 'father of modern chemistry', was a deeply religious man, spending much time over the translation of the Bible into various languages and writing many theological works.[1] John Ray (1627-1705), who laid the foundations of modern botanical and zoological science, also combined a deep religious conviction with a wholehearted allegiance to the methods of observation and experiment, repudiating all the legendary and magical lore with which natural history had hitherto been universally associated; the title of one of his books, *The Wisdom of God in the Works of Creation,* is sufficient indication of his religious attitude.[2] Like Sir Isaac Newton himself, the seventeenth century men of science devoted as much care and attention to theological and biblical reflection as they did to the study of the objects of their scientific interest. The leading thinkers and experimenters of the first phase of the scientific revolution were not only unconscious of any opposition between their scientific attitude and their religious faith but were consciously concerned to express their religious conviction in their scientific work. As far as the origins of modern science are concerned, the notion of a conflict between science and religion is one of the myths of history.

The really significant feature of the scientific revolution of the seventeenth century is that men had begun to look at the world of nature—though not yet at the world of history (or at the Bible)—in a wholly new way, a way entirely unknown to the Greeks, the Hebrews, the Babylonians, the

and Work of a Realist, London, 1959, where a bibliography will be found.
[1] See Roger Pilkington, *Robert Boyle,* London, 1959, for a most readable and valuable study of his life and work.
[2] See Charles E. Raven, *John Ray, Naturalist,* Cambridge, 1942.

Indians, the Chinese, or any other people of ancient or mediaeval times. Much more was involved than the substitution of the Copernican theory for the Ptolemaic; all nature was seen with new eyes. It was not simply that the new facts were brought to light; the significant matter is that the old facts were seen in a new perspective—the facts which were just as accessible to Aristotle as they were to Galileo—bodies falling to the ground, the course of missiles in flight, the impact of moving bodies on stationary ones, the periodic rotation of the heavenly orbs. It was not Aristotle's observations that were at fault, and the mediaevals were constantly enlarging and improving upon them.[1] So long as the Aristotelians thought in terms of invisible teleological movers behind all change, the modern scientific attitude could not arise. To us, who have been born into a scientific civilization, it is almost impossible to appreciate the difficulties encountered by Galileo and his fellows as they attempted to solve the problems which now seem so elementary.[2] The new scientific attitude, the supreme achievement of Christian civilization, is the most important triumph of the human intellect since history began. It has changed the life, the behaviour, the condition and the outlook of men not only in the West but also in what was until recently 'darkest Africa' and the 'changeless East'. If by its conquest of disease it has created new problems of overpopulation and therefore

[1] For an account of mediaeval science, see A. C. Crombie, *Augustine to Galileo: the History of Science, A.D. 400-1650,* London, 1952.
[2] Cf. Herbert Butterfield, *op. cit.,* 2: 'The supreme paradox of the scientific revolution is the fact that things which we find it easy to instil into boys at school, because we see that they start off on the right foot—things which would strike us as the ordinary natural way of looking at the universe, the obvious way of regarding falling bodies, for example—defeated the greatest intellects for centuries, defeated Leonardo da Vinci and at the marginal point even Galileo, when their minds were wrestling on the very frontiers of human thought with these very problems.'

of poverty and starvation, it also holds in its technology and scientific agriculture the only possible solution of these problems. If it has given to the nations new means of aggression which involve the possibility of racial suicide, it has also created the possibility of a unified world-state in which national wars would be an anachronism. If it has put into the hands of a small ruling class the power to control the life and condition the thinking of modern mass-society, it has also made available for the millions the opportunity of broad education and culture, such as in the past were entirely beyond the grasp of the ignorant multitude. Even if the possibility is never realized, science has placed within man's reach the means by which the burdens of poverty, drudgery, disease, ignorance and insecurity may be lifted from the shoulders of mankind. Small wonder that the whole world is willing to accept from the West its Christian inheritance of scientific agriculture, technology and medicine, whatever else it may reject.

It is interesting to ask why this greatest of all revolutions in human thinking should have taken place when it did, and not in any previous age. It was not the work of any one genius, a super-intellect who was responsible for the great advance; it was the achievement of a considerable number of men, who were probably no better endowed with mathematical or inventive genius than other men in previous epochs. It was not even the work of thinkers of any one nation; the great pioneers of the scientific movement came from many countries—Poland, Italy, Denmark, Germany, Holland, France, England. The new ideas leapt rapidly across the bounds of nation and language. It was Hans Lippershey of Middelburg in Holland who in 1608 invented the telescope which inspired Galileo to construct for himself the famous instrument by which he made his startling discoveries, including that of the four satellites of Jupiter, thus undermining the Aristotelian cosmology by shewing that there were some orbs in the solar system which did not revolve round the earth. Why was it that it occurred to so many different people in so many different countries at about the same time that the best way to find out the truth about the universe was not to deduce it from first principles but to discover it through observation and experiment? Whatever may be the full answer to this question, one fact at least is incontrovertible. Natural science arose only in one of the score or so of the great civilizations known to Sir Arnold Toynbee, and that was the Christian civilization—albeit a Christian civilization which had garnered the philosophy and the geometry of Greece, the astronomy of the whole ancient and mediaeval worlds, the arithmetic and algebra of the Indians and Arabs, as well as the religion and ethics of the Hebrews. Natural science and its offspring technology and medicine are the gifts of Christian civilization to mankind. Whether indeed science can flourish in non-Christian civilizations we hardly know, for the Russian experiment has not run long enough as yet; but it would seem that freedom of discussion and enquiry are essential to the progress of science, and that where there is no respect for the person and liberty of the individual it will be science, and not the state, which will wither away.

The question why science arose in Christian civilization (and in no other) has been much discussed. More than thirty years ago A. N. Whitehead argued that faith in the regularity of nature, without which there could be no science, could not have arisen apart from the antecedent faith of mediaeval Christendom in the rationality of God.[1] Belief in the uniformity of nature must have arisen out of (in Whitehead's well-known words) 'the mediaeval insistence on the rationality of God, conceived as with the personal energy of Jehovah and with the rationality of a Greek philosopher.'

[1] A. N. Whitehead, *Science and the Modern World,* London, 1926 (Pelican edition, 1938), Chap. I.

This is perhaps an oversimplification of the matter; the discussion is carried to a deeper level by the suggestion of M. B. Foster that the Christian doctrine of Creation was the source of the non-Greek element which was indispensable to the development of modern science.[1] Only a view of the natural order which takes seriously the freedom of God in creation can give rise to the realization that the contingent regularities of nature must be investigated by observation and experiment and cannot be apprehended by an aristocratic intelligence which expects to find itself at home in a hierarchical rational order. Whatever may be the nature of the connection between Christian theology and the origins of modern science, it can hardly be without significance that the scientific attitude arose in a civilization which acknowledged one God, who was personal, rational and dependable, and that the most ardent and dedicated pioneers of the new scientific movement were themselves devoted students of the Bible and of Christian theology. Still in the future lay the rationalism of the Enlightenment, which gave birth to those positivistic notions that still dominate contemporary philosophy in the English-speaking world, so that it is widely supposed that the only truths which can be known to be true are those which can be verified by the methods of empirical science.

The essentially religious character of the thought of the great seventeenth century scientists appears in their conviction that the ultimate mysteries of the universe and of man's being and destiny were not to be sought in the world of nature. Nor has the enormous progress in scientific knowledge which has been made since their day shewn that they were mistaken. It is a far cry from Galileo's telescope, or

[1] Cf. M. B. Foster's three articles in *Mind* (1934): XLIII, N.S., 446ff.; XLIV, 439ff.; and XLV, 1ff. There is a valuable summary of the whole discussion in E. L. Mascall, *Christian Theology and Natural Science*, London, 1956, 94ff.; see also John Baillie, *Natural Science and the Spiritual Life*, Oxford, 1951, 20f.

from the telescope which Newton made and presented to the Royal Society in 1671, to the wonderful instruments on Mount Wilson and Mount Palomar or at Jodrell Bank; but we have been brought no nearer to solving the ultimate mystery of our existence. This is a subject upon which natural science has nothing to say, since it is beyond the reach of telescopes and microscopes. God is not a term in scientific explanation and therefore science as such has no use for that hypothesis.[1] Nor, if we take the Bible seriously, should we expect science to be able to discover God (cf. Job 11.7). Today our scientific instruments collect information from regions far distant in space; with the aid of a 150 watt transmitter American scientists have sent messages over a distance of eight million miles, and even the Andromeda nebula is not a distant object for Jodrell Bank. But information received from the almost unbelievably remote regions of the universe will not tell us anything more about God than will the ticking of a watch held to the ear. 'Where is the place of understanding? . . . The deep saith, It is not in me, and the sea saith, It is not with me' (Job 28.12, 14).

---

[1] The seventeenth century scientists did not, of course, see this as clearly as we do. Kepler thought that there must be a positive divine force to push the planets round the sky. Newton supposed that certain irregularities in the heavens, which he could not bring under his mathematical formula, must be due to the direct intervention of God. Pierre Simon Laplace (1749-1827), 'the Newton of France', the greatest theoretical astronomer since Newton, solved the mathematical problem which had defeated Newton. This is the meaning of his famous words (alas, probably apocryphal) to Napoleon, who had remarked that he had heard that Laplace had eliminated God from his astronomy: 'Sire, I have no need of that hypothesis.' Laplace was entirely right: God cannot be used as a term in scientific explanation. If we call in God to fill in the 'interstices' of our knowledge, each fresh advance of science will mean that God is being gradually forced out of the universe. The Bible does not encourage us to think of God as a mere *deus ex machina,* to be fallen back upon when other explanations fail; nor can the God of the Bible be made an object of scientific investigation.

Ultimate problems of man's origin and destiny will not be solved by the advance of knowledge in the physical sciences.[1] The world of nature is not the place where 'wisdom' (in the biblical sense) is to be found. Biblical faith has always known this; the pagans might claim to find a revelation of God in the wonders of nature, but concerning a knowledge of God derived from nature the standpoint of the Bible is that of Job 26.14: 'Lo, these are but the outskirts of his ways, and how small a whisper do we hear of him.'

According to the Bible the place in which the revelation of God is to be found is not nature but history. It is only in man and his history that the personal God can be revealed, not in stars and galaxies, crystals and molecules, or even in birds or serpents or four-footed things. It is not Galileo's telescope but Galileo himself who is more likely to provide us with a clue to the riddle of the world: that is why still today people get so worked up about Galileo and the Inquisition.[2] That is why the historian is such an important person even in a scientific and technological civilization. It is why the contents of some jars containing manuscripts written in a dead language, hidden in a cave in the Jordan Valley for perhaps two thousand years, should be instinc-

[1] It is hard to agree that the problems of philosophy and theology will be any nearer solution, as Professor Lovell in his fascinating Reith Lectures seemed to suppose, when our scientific cosmologists are able to tell us whether in fact the physical universe originated at a moment of 'creation' between twenty and sixty thousand million years ago, when a superdense 'primaeval atom' disintegrated, or whether the universe is in a steady state, while within it there is a continuous creation of matter, and stars and galaxies are evolving and disappearing throughout infinite time. (See A. C. B. Lovell, *The Individual and the Universe*, Oxford, 1958, VI.) Christian theology is indifferent as to which of these hypotheses (or neither of them) is correct, because today it is no longer supposed that there is a cosmology revealed in the Bible which may be either proved or disproved by scientific research.

[2] See, e.g., the correspondence in *The Listener* arising out of Professor Lovell's Reith Lectures: 20 Nov. 1958 (Vol. LX, No. 1,547) and the following issues.

tively recognized as an important discovery[1]; it is why the
publication of certain ancient Gnostic texts, discovered in
Upper Egypt in 1946, has been so eagerly awaited.[2] An
antique papyrus roll may perhaps turn out to be no less
important for human existence than the doings of twentieth
century scientists in the Cavendish Laboratory or at Cape
Canaveral. It is only when men have encountered God in his
action in history and have obeyed his word in their hearts
that they recognize, as the Psalmist did, the handiwork of
God in the world of nature (Psalm 19). This word of God in
history is not remote from us, and if we do not hear it in
our own heart we shall not discover it by probing distant
nebulae. 'This commandment . . . is not . . . far off. It is not
in heaven, that thou shouldest say, Who shall go up for us
to heaven, and bring it unto us, and make us to hear it, that
we may do it? . . . But the word is very nigh unto thee, in
thy mouth and in thy heart, that thou mayest do it' (Deut.
30.11-14).

The seventeenth century men of science discerned the
hand of the Creator in the works of nature because they had
encountered the word of the Lord in history and they had
responded to it in faith, obedience and worship. They had
not, indeed, understood the significance of the encounter
with God as *historical* in character, because in this dimension
of their thinking they were still mediaeval. The second stage
of the great scientific revolution which they had initiated still
lay in the future, for the revolution in men's understanding
of history was not accomplished until the nineteenth century.
The 'Age of Reason', which they were entering, did not
understand the significance of history: at best history merely
provides examples and warnings from the past, instructing

[1] See *A Guide to the Scrolls*, ed. A. R. C. Leaney, London, 1958;
J. T. Milik, *Ten Years of Discovery in the Wilderness of Judea*,
London, 1959.
[2] See W. C. van Unnik, *Newly Discovered Gnostic Writings*, London, 1960.

men how to bear themselves prudently in the present; it cannot establish truth, for only reason and experiment can do that.[1] A revolution in men's way of looking at history, comparable to the revolution which had taken place in their way of looking at nature, was necessary before they could perceive the significance of history as the *locus* of man's existential understanding of himself in relation to the world and to God.

[1] Cf. D. G. James, *The Life of Reason,* London, 1949, 49-53, on Thomas Hobbes (1588-1679), in this respect a typical representative of his period. The 'Age of Reason' is generally reckoned to extend from about 1650 to 1780.

2

THE REVOLUTION
IN HISTORICAL THINKING

THE first stage of the scientific revolution was achieved in the seventeenth century, and the year 1687, when Newton's *Principia* appeared, was its hour of triumph. One way of describing its achievement would be to say that the sciences of nature had been emancipated from philosophy and now existed in their own right as independent empirical disciplines. The second stage of the revolution did not occur until the nineteenth century, when scientific method was for the first time seriously applied to man, not merely as a biological organism, but to man and his history, his civilization, social organisation and so on. One way of describing the achievement of the nineteenth century would be to say that history and the human sciences were emancipated from philosophy and now existed in their own right as independent empirical disciplines. The eighteenth century had continued and consolidated the work of its predecessor, but did not significantly advance beyond it. This is not to say that the achievements of the natural scientists of the eighteenth century were inconsiderable. One need only mention the names of Linnaeus (1707-78), who, developing the work of John Ray, laid the foundations of scientific biology by his patient classification of species; of Henry Cavendish (1731-1810), Joseph Priestley (1733-1804) and Antoine Lavoisier (1743-94), who developed the science which we today call chemistry, and which had been liberated by Robert Boyle in the previous century from the toils of alchemy. Although the eighteenth century poet might declare that the proper study of mankind was

THE REVOLUTION IN HISTORICAL THINKING 33

man[1], the almost exclusive object of scientific attention throughout that century was the world of nature. It is not indeed surprising that this should have been so, when there were so many new and exciting lines of investigation to follow up; besides, the realm of nature is so much more accessible to scientific exploration than are the more intractable complexities of human nature.

Nor is it surprising that it should have occurred to the eighteenth century mind that the new mechanistic hypothesis might explain not only the physical universe but the whole realm of mind and spirit as well. But this notion was put forward not by the men of science but by literary men; and it was a philosophical, not a scientific, hypothesis. The *philosophe* movement in France endeavoured to turn the new science into a materialist philosophy. Baron von Holbach or d'Holbach (1723-89) who ran his house in Paris as a salon for advanced thought—so advanced, indeed, that even Rousseau and David Hume felt obliged on occasion to withdraw—published in 1770 his *Système de la Nature* in which the fashionable materialism of the Encyclo-paedists[2] was fully developed. The ancient atomic theory of Democritus and Lucretius was now provided with empirical verification in the discoveries of Newtonian science. Reality was composed of billiard-balls, whether little ones (like atoms) or big ones (like planets), all obeying the Newtonian laws of motion. Living organisms and human brains were only complicated machines, which also obeyed the laws of

[1] Alexander Pope (1688-1744), *Essay on Man*, Ep. ii.
[2] The contributors to the *Encyclopédie,* of which 28 volumes were issued in Paris and (later) Amsterdam between 1751 and 1756, and which in the hands of d'Alembert and Diderot undertook the task of spreading the 'enlightenment' amongst the bourgeoisie. The true philosophy was materialism; religion was superstition; the power of the priests with their miraculous pretensions must be abolished; the privileged classes must be deprived of their economic power; tyrannical government must be reformed, torture abolished, freedom of religion and speech encouraged, etc.

mechanics; everything was thus pre-determined and free-will was an illusion. Since atoms moving about in empty space were the only reality, physics was the universal science and consciousness itself was only an epiphenomenon of matter, like the smell which comes into the room with the pudding and goes out with it. The theory lingered on through the nineteenth century until its 'scientific' basis was destroyed by the rise of quantum physics. Its significance in the history of thought lies in the fact that it seemed to provide an intellectual basis for the suggestion that there was a 'war' between science and religion.

The work of popularizing science for the benefit of the rising new middle class had begun before the end of the seventeenth century. A year before the publication of Newton's *Principia* there had appeared *The Plurality of Worlds* by Bernard Le B. de Fontenelle (1657-1757), who later held the position of secretary of the French Académie des Sciences from 1699 to 1743 and who thus was able to constitute himself a kind of semi-official spokesman of the scientific movement. In his book Fontenelle 'set out to make science amusing to fashionable ladies and as easy as the latest novel'.[1] After him there arose a new class of sophists, who, like Fontenelle, were not themselves men of science but writers and lecturers on topical subjects. Discoursing in the crowded salons of Paris and drawing-rooms of London, to audiences drawn from the socially aspiring new bourgeoisie, upon the latest experiments with magnets or upon the cir-

---

[1] H. Butterfield, *op. cit.,* 149; cf. also 150: 'It is important to note that the great movement of the eighteenth century was a literary one—it was not the new discoveries of science in that epoch but, rather, the French *philosophe* movement that decided the next turn of the story and determined the course Western civilization was to take. The discoveries of seventeenth century science were translated into a new outlook and a new world-view, not by scientists themselves, but by the heirs and successors of Fontenelle.'

culation of the blood, they contrived to suggest that religion was out of date and its foundations mythical. They drew not only upon the new physics but the new geography, for the knowledge of other peoples and cultures in distant lands was increasing rapidly. Other religions besides Christianity claimed to be revealed; heathen nations believed that their traditions and morality rested upon divine authority. The spread of these sceptical and relativistic notions, so strongly in contrast with the intentions and opinions of the men of science themselves, accounts for the apparently paradoxical attitude towards unbelief on the part of the leading Christian apologist of the eighteenth century. Bishop Butler, with his eye on the scientists and their work, can assume without argument the existence of God: 'That there is an intelligent Author of Nature . . . is a principle gone upon in the fore-going treatise, as proved, and generally confessed to be proved.'[1] Similarly, in his Introduction to the *Analogy,* he says that he will take it as 'proved that there is an intelligent Author of Nature and natural Governor of the world, for this has often been proved with accumulated evidence'.[2] Yet with his eye on the new sophists with their middle-class following —a class from which Butler himself had sprung—he writes in the 'Advertisement' prefaced to his first edition (1736): 'It is come, I know not how, to be taken for granted by many persons that Christianity is not so much as a subject of enquiry; but that it is, now at length, discovered to be ficti-tious. And accordingly they treat it as if in the present age this were an agreed point among all people of discernment; and nothing remained but to set it up as a principal subject of mirth and ridicule, as it were by way of reprisals, for its having so long interrupted the pleasures of the world.'

After the religious wars and enthusiasms of the seven-

[1] *The Analogy of Religion, op. cit.,* 143, at the end of his treatment 'Of Natural Religion'.
[2] *Op. cit.,* 6.

teenth century, the eighteenth century was an age of exhaustion. Men turned away from disputes over the content of revelation to the religion of nature, the religion of reason, tolerance and morality. John Tillotson (1630-94), who became Archbishop of Canterbury on the deposition of the non-Juror Sancroft in 1691, had made fashionable the new preaching style of undoctrinal morality, so congenial to the native Pelagianism of Englishmen. The general attitude throughout the eighteenth century was not atheistic but deistic: God was conceived of as an almighty clock-maker, who had constructed the clockwork universe of the scientists, wound up its mechanism and left it running. It was not until the end of the century, after the influence of the French *philosophes* had made itself felt, that it was necessary for Christian apologists, like Archdeacon Paley (1743-1805),[1] to argue that the existence of a watch presupposed the prior existence of a watch-maker (the Argument from Design). The deists apparently believed in a God who, having made the universe and set it going, now took no further interest in it, like a child who has forgotten about a top which he has set spinning. How far this was sometimes only a thinly-veiled atheism is a matter of conjecture.[2] But there was general agreement amongst the deists and their orthodox

---

[1] W. Paley, *Evidences of Christianity* (1794), a work used as a textbook in theological seminaries until well into the present century despite the damage done to its arguments by Darwin's theory of natural selection. Paley drew much of his material from John Ray's *The Wisdom of God Manifested in the Works of the Creation* (1691).

[2] Samuel Clarke (1675-1729), the most influential philosopher and theologian of the earlier eighteenth century, whose correspondence with Leibniz is famous, and with whom Butler as a young man ventured to correspond, wrote in his *Being and Attributes of God* (originally the Boyle lectures of 1704-05) that the deists 'pretend to believe the existence of an eternal, infinite, independent, intelligent Being... (but) they fancy God does not at all concern himself in the government of the world, nor has any regard to, or care of, what is done therein.'

opponents that the true religion was 'the religion of nature', that is, the religion which is grounded upon the truths of reason. In his *Reasonableness of Christianity* (1695) the philosopher John Locke (1632-1704) had argued that the scriptural revelation was acceptable because it was reasonable. Others, like John Toland (1670-1722), who replied to Locke in his *Christianity not Mysterious* (1696), while professing to defend the scriptural revelation, virtually denied the supernatural element in religion altogether; Toland's book was burnt by the public hangman in his native Ireland. The deists maintained that the essential truth about God could be discovered by the 'light of nature,' that is, by reason, and that therefore a religion of revelation was superfluous. The Gospel was at best only a mythological representation of the religion of reason. This is made very clear by the title of the most influential of the treatises produced by the deists, *Christianity as Old as the Creation, or the Gospel a Republication of the Religion of Nature* (1730), by Matthew Tindal (1655-1733). Tindal called himself a 'Christian deist' and his book was known as 'the deist's Bible'; he wrote it as an old man to vindicate the cause for which he had always striven: an earlier work of his had been burned in 1710 by the common hangman by order of the House of Commons. Tindal was able to cite several well known theologians and preachers of the day to shew that they were in essential agreement with his view of the relation of revelation and reason.[1] So commonplace did Tindal's views appear in the 1730s that he was able to sit comfortably in his fellowship at All Souls College, Oxford, until the day of his death at a ripe old age.

[1] Including Samuel Clarke and Thomas Sherlock (1678-1761), then Bishop of Bangor, later of Salisbury and London, who said in a missionary sermon, 'the religion of the Gospel is the true original religion of reason and nature'; it is 'declarative of that original religion which was as old as the creation.' These words of Sherlock's are printed by Tindal on his title-page.

It was Tindal's book which Butler had chiefly in mind when he wrote *The Analogy*. Butler will go as far as he can with the deists, and from our twentieth century point of view that is a very long way. He agrees with them that 'natural religion is the foundation and principal part of Christianity', but, he adds, 'it is not in any sense the whole of it.'[1] Revelation is not superfluous; it informs us of 'somewhat new in the government of the world . . . which could not otherwise have been known.'[2] The thing which most forcibly strikes the present-day reader of *The Analogy,* however, is the almost total absence of any sense of the significance of Christianity as an historical religion, a blind spot which Butler shares with the deists as with almost all eighteenth century theologians. Butler indeed points to the biblical miracles as having really occurred in history, since like all Christian apologists from Aquinas to J. B. Mozley,[3] he holds that apart from such supernatural attestation it would be irrational to believe in the Christian revelation 'upon the mere authority of its author'.[4] Invisible miracles, such as the Incarnation, 'require themselves to be proved by visible miracles. Revelation itself is miraculous, and miracles are the proof of it.'[5] In this sense Christianity is an historical religion; it demands the acknowledgment of the biblical miracles, which attest the truth of the reasonable religion of eighteenth century man. But neither in Butler nor in his contemporaries is there any awareness at all that the heart of biblical religion is the proclamation of the saving acts of God in history, or that Christianity began as the proclamation of an historical event and not as the republication of the religion of nature. The

[1] *Op. cit.,* 154.
[2] *Op. cit.,* 163.
[3] *Eight Lectures on Miracles* (Bampton Lectures, 1865), 31f. See on this subject Alan Richardson, *Christian Apologetics* (1947), 154-61.
[4] *Op. cit.,* 284.
[5] *Op. cit.,* 174.

reason why the significance of the historical element in Christianity was not appreciated was that the eighteenth century possessed almost no sense of the importance of history. The world of nature, not the world of man, was the all-engrossing object of the attention of the men of the Enlightenment.

It was not only the theologians who in the eighteenth century were deficient of a sense of history. In the Age of Reason it was natural to suppose that only universals and not particular historical instances should possess significance. As the German philosopher and man of letters G. E. Lessing (1729-81) insisted, 'Incidental truths of history can never become the proof of necessary truths of reason'.[1] Accordingly he rejected the idea of revelation altogether and made a noble humanitarian ethic the essence of religion.[2] Similarly the French *philosophe* movement, with its theory that atoms in motion were the only reality and that therefore physical science was the proper instrument for the investigation of human motives and behaviour, had no understanding of the importance of the study of history. J. S. Mill in his Essay on Coleridge (1840)[3] remarked that the eighteenth century mind undervalued the past because it did not understand it; it 'anathematized all that had been going on in Europe from Constantine ... to Voltaire' and could not think rightly about the present because it had not done justice to the past. Mill remarks that the disrespect in which history was held by the *philosophes* is notorious, and he quotes by way of illustration d'Alembert's wish that 'all record whatever of past

---

1   Henry Chadwick, *Lessing's Theological Writings,* London, 1956, 53; cf. also 31.
2   The philanthropic, tolerant and enlightened Jew who is the chief character in Lessing's play, *Nathan der Weise* (1779), embodies an eighteenth century ideal. Despite his rejection of Christianity as an historical religion, Lessing's work *Die Erziehung des Menschengeschlechts* (1780) laid the foundation of the dominant German Liberal Protestantism of the nineteenth century.
3   *Mill on Bentham and Coleridge,* ed. by F. R. Leavis (1950), 128f.

events could be blotted out'. Of course, Mill is no less aware than any of the deists or *philosophes* that an uncomprehending veneration of past formulations of beliefs and types of behaviour is a clinging to dead forms, a fossilization of what had once been a living and growing faith. But Mill stands, as they did not, on the further side of the revolution in men's attitude to history, and he knows that man, as distinct from atoms, cannot be understood apart from his history. He rightly sees that S. T. Coleridge (1772-1834) is in an important sense the prophet of a new age, or at least one of the signs of its dawning, an age which was to appreciate in a wholly new way the significance of history. Despite its veneration of natural science, the eighteenth century had little conception of what is involved in the scientific investigation of human history and society. It admired theoretical reconstructions of human institutions, such as J.J.Rousseau's famous *Contrat Social* (1762), but it never occurred to the mind of the eighteenth century that the assumptions upon which it was based—such as that human nature is fundamentally good, that primitive man was a free and happy creature living in accordance with his natural instincts, and that he had been corrupted only by his institutions—could be made the object of disinterested scientific empirical investigation.[1]

[1] The 'pre-historical' age before the nineteenth century had, of course, no conception that man and his social institutions had in any way evolved from a lower to a higher level of existence; cf. John Dryden (1631-1701):

> I am as free as Nature first made man,
> Ere the base laws of servitude began,
> When wild in woods the noble savage ran.

The 'noble savage', untrammelled by human institutional encumbrances, was guided by reason, 'the pure light of nature', and followed the dictates of his conscience in truly human nobility, before the 'prejudices' (as the Christian doctrines of Original Sin or man's need of Redemption were called by the men of the Enlightenment) had been made into fetters for his soul.

The truth is that the mediaeval world-view did not disintegrate in all its parts at equal speed. Long after the triumph of the Newtonian physics and cosmology, the mediaeval attitude to history continued its unchallenged reign. A revolution in the sphere of history, comparable to that which had taken place in the sphere of natural science in the seventeenth century, did not occur until the nineteenth century. The men of the seventeenth and eighteenth centuries lived in two overlapping worlds—the modern world of physical science and the mediaeval world of history. Sir Isaac Newton himself is the perfect illustration of the man who is half modern, half mediaeval. The greatest scientific genius of an age of brilliant discoverers, the President of the Royal Society and the acknowledged leader of the new scientific movement, devoted hours of sedulous research to the task of synchronizing the observed phenomena of the heavenly bodies with the chronology of the Bible as the late mediaeval world understood it. Newton's *Principia Mathematica* is one of the supreme achievements of the modern mind: his *Observations on the Prophecies of Daniel and the Apocalypse of St John,* published posthumously in 1733, is a work of almost undiluted mediaeval scholasticism. Indeed, the mediaeval scheme of world-chronology had in Newton's day recently received its classic and final formulation at the hands of James Ussher. Ussher, who became Archbishop of Armagh in 1625, besides being a very fine scholar, was one of the most attractive characters in an age of bitter religious strife; so admired were his scholarship and his charity alike that he was accorded a State funeral by Oliver Cromwell in 1656. Ussher's *Annales Veteris et Novi Testamenti* (1650-4) remained the standard scheme of world chronology until the rise of biblical historical science in the nineteenth century. From this work were taken the dates which since 1701 were regularly inserted in the margins of the Authorized Version (or King James Version) of the Bible: the Creation, 4004 B.C.;

the Flood, 2349; the Exodus, 1491, B.C., and so on.[1] It is difficult for us, who live on this side of the nineteenth century revolution in historical method, to put ourselves into the position of those who lived before it. It is hard today even for a schoolboy to understand why so great a genius as Galileo was never quite able to make up his mind whether heavier bodies fell to the ground sooner than lighter ones; it is equally hard for us to understand why such fine scholars as James Ussher and John Lightfoot never discovered a soundly historical view of human development.

The eighteenth century did not develop a scientific conception of history for the same reason that the scholastic philosophers of the Middle Ages did not develop a scientific attitude to the world of nature; in both cases men's minds were dominated by an authoritative tradition, a received perspective, which had to be transcended before the new method and new perspective could be attained. In both cases what had to be outgrown was the classical tradition or perspective, the legacy of Greece.[2] The Greeks had no conception of development in history; for them history was cyclical, and their golden age was in the past. Though modified in the Christian era by its having been uneasily united with the biblical view of history as linear, and as having a beginning and an ending, the classical view of history dominated the mind of the seventeenth and eighteenth century and prevented the emergence of any conception of a real develop-

[1] A fine Cambridge scholar, John Lightfoot (1602-75), whose *Horae Hebraicae et Talmudicae* in six volumes exhibits a truly astonishing range of biblical, rabbinic and linguistic scholarship, reasoned on the basis of the contemporary view of world history that the actual creation of man took place on October 23rd, 4004 *B.C.*, at 9 a.m. Once again we see illustrated the truth that advance in science depends not only, and not primarily, upon the accumulation of new facts, but upon seeing the well known facts in a new perspective.

[2] Cf. the very suggestive introduction to *The Greek Historians*, edited by M. I. Finley, London, 1959.

ment in history or of real changes in man's condition. Primitive man was a 'noble savage' who lived according to nature, that is, reason; or, as Robert South (1634-1716), the Public Orator of Oxford and a Canon of Christ Church, remarked in a sermon, 'An Aristotle was but the rubbish of an Adam, and Athens but the rudiments of paradise.' The history of mankind from Adam to Aristotle, as from Constantine to Voltaire, was but decline and fall. In Gibbon's famous phrase, history was 'little more than the register of the crimes, follies and misfortunes of mankind'.[1] For Gibbon the golden age of history was the age of the Antonines: 'If a man were called to fix the period in the history of the world during which the condition of the human race was most happy and prosperous, he would, without hesitation, name that which elapsed from the death of Domitian to the accession of Commodus.'[2] In view of the monumental greatness of the chief historical work of the eighteenth century, the *Decline and Fall* by Edward Gibbon (1737-94), based as it was upon a study of the original materials and of the writings of the French and Italian historians—Tillemont, J. Mabillon, B. Montfaucon and L. A. Muratori—it would be absurd to say that the eighteenth century knew nothing about history and cared nothing—just as it would be absurd to say that the late mediaeval schoolmen of the Aristotelian-Ptolemaic tradition knew nothing about astronomy and physics. It is a question of perspective and of scientific attitude and method. In the seventeenth and eighteenth centuries history had not yet won its independence from philosophy as a discipline that should and could exist in its own right. Even to this statement certain qualifications should perhaps be added, for in the work of the French historians there is found some anticipation of the nineteenth century attitude; Voltaire's *L'Histoire de Charles XII* (1731) is sometimes

[1] *Decline and Fall of the Roman Empire*, Chap. 3.
[2] *Ibid.*

said to have inaugurated the modern technique of historical investigation. Voltaire (1694-1778) had certainly begun to think of history as the story of man, his civilization and morals, rather than of monarchs and their wars. But, by and large, it is true to say that before the nineteenth century history was not written by 'historians' but by philosophers and literary men with an axe to grind. Thus, the *Discours sur l'histoire universelle* (1681) by the French preacher and Bishop of Meaux, J.B. Bossuet (1627-1704), was written for the edification of the dauphin, the son of Louis XIV, and aimed at shewing how all the ancient empires were divinely ordained stages in the providential progress of mankind towards its true destiny, the Catholic Church. Gibbon, on the other hand, wrote his *magnum opus* to prove the precisely opposite point of view: the Middle Ages represented 'the triumph of barbarism and religion', and the Holy Roman Empire and indeed the Catholic Church itself constituted but a squalid and dreary interlude between the golden age of the Antonines and the enlightened Age of Reason. History was made the handmaid of philosophical and polemical writing; it served chiefly 'to point a moral or adorn a tale'. Bossuet and Gibbon stand on the mediaeval side of the revolution in historical method.

In the eighteenth century the educated classes in England had not formed the habit of reading history. They had, of course, read the ancient historians—Herodotus, Thucydides, Xenophon, Plutarch, Caesar, Livy and Tacitus; and they had perhaps learnt something of English history from the chronicles of Stow, Hall or Holinshed—or from the historical plays of Shakespeare, who had quarried his materials from the same sources. There were a few accounts of recent events, such as Clarendon's *History of the Rebellion* (published posthumously in 1702) and Burnet's *History of My Own Times* (1723-4), a few histories of the Reformation (including one by Burnet), and so on. It was the philosopher

David Hume who composed the first extended *History of England* (six volumes, 1754-61), beginning with the Roman occupation; it was written from a Tory viewpoint, and it was (unlike its author's philosophical works) an immediate success; it retained its popularity as the standard English history until the publication of John Richard Green's *Short History of the English People* in 1874. Between 1776 and 1787 the six volumes of Gibbon appeared; after the turn of the nineteenth century the quiet stream of historical writing became a broad, swiftly flowing river, which by the middle of the century had become a flood. All at once the educated public became history-conscious, and the spate of new works, dealing with various periods of history, could scarcely meet the demand. Literary men became good historians and wrote readable and on the whole accurate history. Various epochs of the past were 'rediscovered'; the Middle Ages, Gibbon's age of 'barbarism and religion', became a magic age of mystery and romance, and classical architecture yielded place to the Gothic revival.[1] The historical novel was found to be a convenient means of satisfying the new thirst for knowledge of the past: Sir Walter Scott's *Waverley* appeared in 1814 and the series of 'Waverley Novels' followed in rapid succession. Men of action, like Edward Bulwer (Lord Lytton, 1803-73), joined the literary men in the production of this new and stimulating form of imaginative historical writing.[2] Artists painted historical scenes, often on vast canvases. The list of historical works which appeared during the first half

---

[1] Cf. Max Beerbohm's comment upon Victorian railway-station architecture: '... the fading signals and grey eternal walls of that antique station, which, familiar to them and insignificant, does yet whisper to the tourist the last enchantments of the Middle Age' (*Zuleika Dobson*, 1911, opening paragraph). Beerbohm is parodying a phrase from M. Arnold, *Essays in Criticism,* first series, Preface.

[2] *The last Days of Pompeii* appeared in 1834, *Rienzi* in 1835, and many less well known novels and plays followed.

of the nineteenth century is far too long to catalogue, but mention should be made of Carlyle's *French Revolution* (1837) and Macaulay's *History of England,* the first volume of which appeared in 1848.

All this literary activity was, however, only one aspect of the change which had occurred in men's way of looking at the past. A less tangible but not less real revolution than the 'Copernican' was taking place about the beginning of the nineteenth century, and it did not concern the world of nature but the world of man. As with the seventeenth century revolution in men's way of looking at nature, so in the nineteenth century the revolution in men's way of looking at history involved a complete break with tradition, a rejection of the classical outlook and of the whole mediaeval scheme of world-chronology. Until the close of the eighteenth century the European mind had been dominated by the classic view of history as static, of ages of degeneration (such as the mediaeval period) following upon a Golden Age of peace and prosperity, and then being succeeded by a return to the pristine order of things, which was 'the order of nature'. This is an essentially cyclical view of history; no really new order of things has arisen or will arise; there is only a recurrence of ages of decay and of restoration. As Marcus Aurelius expressed the classical view, a man of forty years of age has seen all that has ever been or ever shall be. In strong contrast to this outlook the nineteenth century attained the conception of real change in history; and if its idea of 'progress' was often altogether too optimistic and too unsophisticated, it was at least an understandable outcome of the new sense of historical development, of a real evolution in the condition and thought of the human race during the period of recorded history. As with the scientific revolution of the seventeenth century, it is hard to give reasons why the historical revolution should have occurred when it did; but one obvious cause is not far to seek. That other revolution, itself largely a consequence of the scientific revolution, namely, the industrial revolution, was already in the early decades of the nineteenth century rapidly altering the human condition and visibly changing age-old ways of living and working. The first half of the nineteenth century had witnessed a greater change in the human scene than had ever taken place in the whole span of recorded history; and, of course, the awareness and indeed expectation of change has increased with every succeeding decade right up to our own days. A new outlook upon man's history and possibilities was inevitable as the age of horse locomotion gave place to the age of steam and all that has followed it. To learn how intensely the nineteenth century mind itself was aware of the changing condition and face of England it is necessary only to read the opening chapters of Macaulay's *History*.

The historical revolution in its turn reacted upon nineteenth century philosophy, political thought and action, and even upon development in the natural sciences themselves, especially the biological ones. Of its impact upon theology we shall speak in the next chapter. G. W. F. Hegel (1770-1831), who became Professor of Philosophy in Berlin in 1818, dominated philosophical thought on the Continent during the first half of the century and in England during the second half of it. He expounded an essentially evolutionary view of the universe, according to which the logic of world-history was inexorably realizing itself through the dialectical process of thesis, antithesis and synthesis; he brought all aspects of human experience—scientific, aesthetic, legal, political and religious—under his rational law of logical evolution. The scientific philosophy of the latter part of the century, such as the naturalism of Herbert Spencer and T. H. Huxley, though repudiating Hegel's idealism, was no less confidently evolutionary: 'it is certain,' said Spencer, 'that man must become perfect.' Political philosophers and economists also made use of the new evolutionary idea. Karl

Marx (1818-1883), who 'stood Hegel on his head,' took over from him the idea of the dialectical movement of history, using the concept of economic determinism to prove 'scientifically' the necessity of the final appearance of the classless society, the goal of the evolutionary process. This secularized Messianism was presented to the world in *Das Kapital* (Vol. I, 1867), which became the Scripture of nineteenth century revolutionary socialism. The new historical attitude also conditioned the way in which the nineteenth century looked at the world of organic nature and rendered it possible to regard nature itself from the new evolutionary point of view. Charles Darwin (1809-1882) is popularly supposed to have been the originator of the idea of biological evolution, but, of course, the theory had been put forward long before he and Alfred Russel Wallace (1823-1913) had presented to the historic meeting of the Linnean Society (July 1st, 1858) their joint paper which detailed the empirical evidence disproving the time-honoured doctrine of the immutability of species.[1] Already in 1844 an anonymous work entitled *The Vestiges of Creation* had appeared in the form of a popular handbook of natural science, which put forward the evolutionary theory of human origins. It created considerable interest and discussion, and there was much speculation about its authorship; it was widely attributed to the Prince Consort. But its author was a Scottish publisher, Robert Chambers (1802-71), a devout theist who believed that the theory of evolution supported the Argument from Design. What Darwin and Wallace actually did was to provide the empirical evidence which the theory had hitherto lacked; incidentally, the Darwinian hypothesis of natural selection, or the survival of the fittest, which long remained a matter of dispute among biologists, dealt a severe blow to the Argument from Design,

[1] See Bentley Glass, Owsei Temkin and William L. Straus Jr. (editors), *Forerunners of Darwin, 1745-1859,* John Hopkins Press and O.U.P., London, 1959.

as Paley had formulated it. The publication of Darwin's *Origin of Species* (1859) caused less outcry than that of *The Vestiges of Creation* had done, although public attention was somewhat theatrically drawn to the issue by the memorable altercation between the Bishop of Oxford (Samuel Wilberforce) and T. H. Huxley at the meeting of the British Association in 1860. Happily there were more thoughtful churchmen than Wilberforce, who perceived already that the protagonists were skirmishing over a side-issue. They saw that the real issue concerning the truth of revelation lay not in biological research, even research into human biology, but in history, where the crucial battle was going on. Darwin's *Origin of Species,* as thoughtful Christians like R.W. Church recognized at the time, was no more inimical to the revelation in Christ than Newton's *Principia Mathematica* had been. The truth of this perception was symbolized by the burial of Darwin close by Isaac Newton's grave in Westminster Abbey in 1882.[1]

The real challenge of the nineteenth century revolution in human thinking lay not in the realm of natural science but in the realm of history. In the opening decades of the century the new historical methods, now being taught and practised in Germany by Leopold von Ranke, who became Professor of History at Berlin in 1825, and others of the 'scientific' school of historians, were inevitably applied to the Bible and to Christian origins. As usual, there were those who were

[1] It may be useful to remind ourselves how the episode appears from the perspective of contemporary rationalism. Mr Hesketh Pearson recently wrote in *The Spectator* (20 Nov. 1959, 696): 'While I was writing his (i.e. Henry Labouchere's) life in 1935, I happened one day to be discussing the whole question of institutionalism with Malcolm Muggeridge. I remember we laughed heartily over the fact that Charles Darwin, whose evolutionary theories had horrified the Church of England in 1859, was yet buried in Westminster Abbey twenty-three years later; and we concluded that the Church had quickly adapted the Book of Genesis to the new revelation.'

ready at once to employ the new science in the attack upon traditional Christian belief. In the hands of the rationalistic school of Tübingen the new historical approach led rapidly to the scepticism of D. F. Strauss, who in his notorious *Leben Jesu* (1835-6) argued that the supernatural element in the Gospels was a 'myth' entirely without historical foundation, having grown up during the long interval between the days of Jesus himself and the middle of the second century, when the Gospels were written. Not unnaturally it seemed to the conservatively minded that 'biblical criticism'—that is, the application of scientific historical method to the literature of the Bible—must necessarily be 'destructive'; to any Christian believer, who was alive to the challenge of the new historical thinking, the question became all at once cruelly urgent. The abyss of historical scepticism had been terrifyingly uncovered. The two most sensitively religious minds of the nineteenth century, John Henry Newman (1801-90) and Søren Kierkegaard (1813-55), illustrated two quite different forms of reaction to the terror of the abyss. Newman, recoiling in horror from the yawning chasm of doubt, sought the security of an infallible dogmatic authority; Kierkegaard, in shuddering dread yet strangely revelling in the sensation of vertigo, essayed to pass over the chasm by means of the 'leap of faith'. Different though their reactions were, both Newman and Kierkegaard acutely perceived the challenge of the new historical thinking to the Christian assertion of a revelation in history.

Newman, comforting himself with the strange theory that the scepticism of Strauss was the natural 'development' of Luther's doctrine of justification by faith,[1] was too good an historian to acquiesce for long in the pious belief of the older

---

[1] *Essay on the Development of Christian Doctrine* (ed. 1878, 193). Strauss's *Life of Jesus* was translated into English by Miss Barber and George Eliot and published in 1846, the year after Newman's reception into the Roman Church.

THE REVOLUTION IN HISTORICAL THINKING 51

Anglican divines (and of his former Tractarian colleagues) in the immutability of Christian doctrine down the ages.[1] His *Essay on the Development of Christian Doctrine* (1845) represents the unresolved perplexity of one who, fleeing from 'the open infidelity of Strauss', must reconcile the official Roman view that after all the apostles were dead there could be no further revelation[2] with the historian's knowledge that Catholic doctrine had in fact been 'developing' during eighteen centuries of growth.[3]

Kierkegaard, like Newman, fought a lonely battle with scepticism in the innermost depths of his own being. His reply to the objection of the eighteenth century mind,[4] that eternal truth cannot be disclosed in the particular truths of history, is that the human understanding must learn that there are paradoxes which it cannot 'understand'—for instance, that the eternal has been revealed in history. Paradox is not poetic half-truth, nor yet confession of ignorance, but a category of rational explanation. It is the ontological expression of a relationship between a real person (Kierke-

---

1 Newman knew well enough that there had been a 'development' of doctrine both before and after the Council of Nicea, and hence he could not remain satisfied with such time-honoured apologies as that of George Bull, Bishop of St David's, in his *Defensio Fidei Nicenae* (1685). The High Anglican Bishop had defended the orthodoxy of the pre-Nicene Fathers against the Jesuit, D. Petavius (or Petau), who charged them with 'Platonism'; Bull had received the approbation of Bishop Bossuet and a vote of thanks from a Synod of French clergy in 1686. But Newman remarks that 'out of the thirty (pre-Nicene) writers whom he (Bull) reviews, he has, for one cause or another, to "explain piously" about twenty' (*Essay, ed. cit.,* 134).

2 Reaffirmed in 1907 by the decree of the Holy Office, *Lamentabili,* which condemned sixty-five propositions associated with the outlook of the Roman Catholic 'Modernists'.

3 On this whole theme see **Owen Chadwick**, *From Bossuet to Newman,* Cambridge, 1957.

4 As voiced, e.g., by Lessing: see the quotation on page 39 above. Kierkegaard restates the objection on the title page of the *Philosophical Fragments* (1844).

gaard's 'individual existent') and eternal truth. Truth, essential and eternal, as distinct from the contingent 'truths' of the empirical sciences or of everyday common-sense, is vitally related to persons who are engaged existentially in the struggle for obedience to God's will in the everyday business of living. It is discovered, or rather 'revealed', in the passionate inwardness (subjectivity) of 'one who exists' and hence is related to existence (i.e. to persons) only paradoxically. This paradoxical relationship of the individual to eternal truth is called faith. Faith is the instrument of the individual's apprehension of history, or, in its more specifically Christian sense, the apprehension of revelation in historical events. It is not the conclusion of a process of reasoning but a decision, and one which involves the possibility of error: no one learns to swim who will not take the plunge until he is sure that he can swim. Faith is the acceptance of paradox in all its absurdity. The 'absolute paradox', or basic absurdity, is that the Eternal Truth has entered the process of becoming (history), that God has been born an infant, grown up like other people, and has worn our clothes and spoken our language so perfectly that it is possible to mistake him for a man like other men. In this matter the contemporaries of Jesus enjoyed no advantages over those who live eighteen centuries after him; the knowledge of the historical details concerning him, which they possessed and which we labour critically to 'reconstruct', are quite irrelevant to the understanding of the paradox. Faith can be neither verified nor refuted by historical science. The apostolic witnesses did all that was needful to call the attention of subsequent generations to the paradox of God's becoming man; indeed, they did 'more than enough'. It is not the writers of the New Testament in their capacity of reliable historians who bring men to faith; it is God himself who brings men in every generation (including that of Jesus's contemporaries) into that subjective relationship with the eternal truth which

is called faith, and thus every generation is equally contemporaneous with the revelation in Christ. We can have
historical knowledge about the Jesus of history, but the
Christ of God, the Paradox itself, is accessible only to faith:
'about him nothing can be known; he can only be believed.'
Here, in a word, is Kierkegaard's answer to the historical
scepticism of Strauss: 'If the contemporary generation had
left nothing behind them but these words: "We have believed
that in such and such a year God appeared among us in the
humble figure of a servant, that he lived and taught in our
community, and finally died," it would be more than enough.
The contemporary generation would have done all that was
necessary; for this little advertisement, this *nota bene* on a
page of universal history, would be sufficient to afford an
occasion for a successor, and the most voluminous account
can in all eternity do nothing more.'[1]

[1] *Philosophical Fragments,* translation by David F. Swenson, Oxford and New York, 1936, 87.

3

THE REVOLUTION
IN THEOLOGICAL THINKING

HOWEVER we account for the fact, the study of history in the sense in which we understand it today, like the pursuit of empirical science, is an achievement of Christian civilization. To say this is not to disparage Herodotus, who has long been accorded the honorific title of 'the father of history,' or any of the other great literary 'historians' of Greece and Rome, or, for that matter, the writers of the 'historical' books of the Old Testament. Of course there were historians and chroniclers both in the ancient and in the mediaeval worlds, and much of our knowledge of the past is derived from them. Again, as in the case of science, there is no need to quarrel about words. What we are speaking about is the modern conception of *critical* history, or 'scientific history' as it is sometimes called.[1] This involves both a critical attitude towards sources, which may thus be made to yield very different information from what their writers intended to convey, and also a determination to seek the truth for its own sake and not for the sake of demonstrating some preconceived dogmatic opinion. The achievement of

[1] The term 'scientific history', however, has come into disfavour in some quarters because of its association with extreme notions about the possibility of attaining a thoroughly objective or impartial historical perspective, comparable to the objectivity attainable in the natural sciences. It is widely admitted today that 'presuppositionless' history is an illusion: nevertheless the historian should try to criticize his own presuppositions and prejudices and to be as 'impartial' as he can. See on this subject Alan Richardson, *Christian Apologetics*, Chap. IV.

this ideal involves looking at the past from an entirely new perspective, comparable to the new way of looking at nature which the rise of empirical scientific method had involved. The historical revolution which was consummated in the nineteenth century was, as we have suggested, just as radical a break with past attitudes as was the scientific revolution of the seventeenth century. The careful, disciplined and sustained study of man's history was a new enterprise of the human spirit, something which had not been envisaged in classical or mediaeval times: Plato's Academy did not teach history, and Aristotle never engaged in historical research.

There can be no doubt that the break up of the unity of western Christendom at the Reformation was indirectly a powerful stimulus to the study of history in the modern period. Each of the confessions, Catholic and Protestant, Lutheran and Reformed, Anglican and Dissenter, Arminian and Socinian, developed the appeal to history in its polemic against the others. Each appealed to a supposed immutable dogmatic tradition which supported its case. The main field of historical study in the earlier modern period was thus that of ecclesiastical history and the history of dogma. But this was hardly yet historical study in the sense of modern critical history; its motive was apologetic and polemical rather than genuinely 'scientific'. Nevertheless interest in the past was awakened, and it was inevitable that sooner or later, as the zeal for controversy waned, a desire to understand the past for its own sake should arise. The credit for the earliest development of the spirit of pure enquiry should probably go to the Maurists,[1] who esteemed scholarship for its own

---

[1] The French Benedictine monks of the Congregation of St-Maur, founded in 1621. By 1685 six of their 180 monasteries, ruled by a Superior-General from St Germain-des-Prés, Paris, had concentrated within them a remarkable band of scholars engaged in various forms of literary and historical research. Towards the end of the eighteenth century the Congregation had begun to decline; the Superior-General and many others were victims of

sake as a means of discipline and as a vocation by which God was to be glorified in much the same way as other monastic orders had esteemed manual labour in the field, kitchen or hospital. They have rightly been called the first 'historians', because they gave to the world the ideal of scholarship for its own sake, and not for the sake of polemic, whether it be that of a Bossuet or a Gibbon. In the work of Jean Mabillon (1632-1707), who may be said to have founded the science of diplomatic and to be the father of critical mediaeval history, the disinterested quest for historical knowledge had definitely emerged upon the modern scene. When the Romantic Movement arose to extend interest beyond the range of ecclesiastical history to the wider spheres of secular history at large, the example and the methods of the Maurists were ready to hand.

The movement known as Romanticism, which ushered in the nineteenth century, brought with it a new interest in and a new sense of history as real change and as significant development. Its theological expression took quite different forms in Germany and in England. In Germany Friedrich Schleiermacher (1768-1834) with his theology of 'religious experience' dominated the nineteenth century scene and truly founded an epoch, but it was not until the later years of the century that his influence had spread to Britain. In England there was no comparable systematic theologian to re-state the theology of revelation in the light of the revolution in historical method, and we have to look rather to the poets for the religious expression of Romanticism: Wordsworth's *Excursion* is the supreme example. S. T. Coleridge (1772-1834), it is true, exercised a subtle influence upon the development of theology in the nineteenth century, but he was not a systematic thinker either in the sphere of theology or in that of philosophy. He was in no sense an English Schleier-

the guillotine in 1789, and the Congregation was finally suppressed by Pope Pius VII in 1818.

macher, but he was acutely aware of the need for a reformulation of the traditional doctrine of scriptural revelation in the light of the new historical knowledge; J. S. Mill expressed the fear that 'the rising generation of Tories and Highchurchman' should find him 'vastly too liberal'.[1] 'He bewails "bibliolatry" as the pervading error of modern Protestant divinity, and the great stumbling-block of Christianity, and exclaims, "O might I live but to utter all my meditations on this most concerning point . . . in what sense the Bible may be called the word of God, and how and under what conditions the unity of the Spirit is translucent through the letter, which, read as the letter merely, is the word of this and that pious, but fallible and imperfect man." '[2]

In these words Coleridge poses the question which English biblical scholars in the nineteenth century set themselves to answer. They approached the question not from the more ambitious angle of systematic theology, as Schleiermacher did, but along the more empirical, more pedestrian (or more *English*) avenue of the critical study of the Bible itself. We shall postpone till the next chapter our consideration of the development of continental theology from Schleiermacher to Karl Barth, since it is more convenient to follow the two different lines of approach one at a time; in the remainder of this chapter we shall trace the course of English scholarly opinion up to the time when, a decade or so after World War I, Barth's impact upon it was forcibly felt. But before we deal with the central issue, one incidental matter of some importance should be noticed. The parallel with the rise of natural science and its interconnection with theological insight is a close one. We remarked in the first chapter that scientific methods and discoveries were not forced upon

[1] F. R. Leavis, *op. cit.*, 166.
[2] *Ibid.* 165f. The quotation is from the *Literary Remains,* iv.6; see also the *Confessions of an Inquiring Spirit* (recently edited by H. St J. Hart, London, 1956).

Christian thought by some non-Christian investigators oper-
ating from outside the Christian world-view: they were, on
the contrary, developed by devout Christian minds who were
unanimous in the conviction that they were serving that God
of truth whose self-revelation had been given to the world
in the Bible. Similarly the historical revolution of the nineteenth century was not an alien, untheological necessity
forced upon unwilling Christian scholars from the outside:
on the contrary, the development of the critical historical
method was itself largely the work of clergymen who, like
the monks of St-Maur, had become convinced that the
integrity of their devotion to the God of truth constrained
them to follow their critical studies to the very end of the
scholarly road. As with the scientific revolution of the seventeenth century, so with the historical revolution of the nineteenth: there was fundamentally no conflict between 'science'
and 'religion', at least at the top levels of thought, because
the investigators were themselves men of deep Christian
conviction. The outcry, when it arose—as after the publication of *Essays and Reviews* in 1860—was raised by those
who had not participated in the researches of the scholars
and did not understand either their motives or their conclusions. As with the natural sciences, it was not in the
Universities that the new methods of historical study were
developed in England.[1] It is true that in 1724 George II had
established Regius Professorships of Modern History at
Oxford and Cambridge, but their duties were to supervise
the language studies of suitable young men for the diplomatic
service, since these were in short supply.[2] In 1841 Thomas
Arnold, a fine classical scholar, was appointed to the chair

[1]   At Cambridge, more forward in natural science than Oxford, a
       chair of Mathematics was established only in 1663, of Experi-
       mental Philosophy in 1704, of Chemistry in 1713, of Zoology in
       1866, seven years after the publication of *The Origin of Species*.
[2]   E. L. Woodward, *British Historians,* London, 1943, 10.

at Oxford while still Headmaster of Rugby, and he lectured on Roman history, but also occasionally upon modern history, until his premature death in the following year. William Stubbs, who later became Bishop successively of Chester and Oxford, was the first historian in the modern sense to become Professor of Modern History at Oxford (from 1866 to 1884), and he had laid the foundations of his immense historical erudition in his country living of Navestock in Essex (1850-66). Mandell Creighton, later to become Bishop of London, had likewise developed his historical studies in the far-away Merton College living of Embleton on the coast of Northumberland, before he became the first Dixie Professor of Ecclesiastical History at Cambridge (in 1884) and the first editor of the *English Historical Review*. E. A. Freeman, who succeeded Stubbs as Regius Professor at Oxford, wrote the five volumes of his *History of the Norman Conquest* (1867-76) at his country home in Somerset.[1]

In the sphere of biblical studies the new critical historical methods only slowly won their way into the Universities. The original Tractarians agreed with Newman in deprecating not only the conclusions but also the methods which were being favoured across the German Ocean. E. B. Pusey, who was Regius Professor of Hebrew at Oxford from 1828 until his death in 1882, had studied in Göttingen and Berlin shortly after he was elected a Fellow of Oriel (1823). He published *An Historical Enquiry into the Probable Causes of the Rationalist Character lately dominant in the Theology of Germany* (1828-30), but later withdrew it when he found

[1] Cambridge had no equivalents to the great Oxford historians of the second half of the nineteenth century, Stubbs, Freeman, John Richard Green and J. A. Froude, until in 1895 Lord Acton became Regius Professor. Acton, educated on the Continent under Döllinger, had already effectively demonstrated the value of the critical historical method in his contributions to the *English Historical Review*, etc.

it was misunderstood as a defence of the new ways; there-after he consistently opposed the critical approach to the Bible. Other prominent and influential high churchmen exercised a strongly conservative influence in Oxford, amongst them J. W. Burgon (1813-88), Fellow of Oriel (1846) and Vicar of the University Church, subsequently Dean of Chichester, and H. P. Liddon (1829-90), who in 1870 was appointed Dean Ireland's Professor of Biblical Exegesis and also Canon of St Paul's. They viewed with dismay the rising tide of liberal thought, which demanded the reform of the Universities and the freeing of them from clerical control and ecclesiastical restrictions; as they rightly perceived, it would inevitably open the gates to the new and dangerous modern ideas and methods. Nor were they re-assured, when the Royal Commission to enquire into the state of Oxford University was set up in 1850, to find that its secretary was A. P. Stanley (1815-81), subsequently Dean of Westminster (1864), a broad churchman who advocated liberal policies and admired contemporary German theology. The storm broke in 1860 with the publication of *Essays and Reviews*. The seven essayists, six of whom were clergymen, believed in the necessity of freedom in theological enquiry and held that the time had come to explain the new approach to biblical and theological questions to the educated public. The attack on the volume of essays was led by Samuel Wilberforce, then Bishop of Oxford; and two of the essayists, R. Williams and H. B. Wilson, were saved from deprivation of their benefices only by the intervention of the Judicial Committee of the Privy Council. Eleven thousand clergymen signed a protest, affirming their belief in the inspiration of the Scriptures and in eternal punishment. As R. W. Church remarked to Asa Gray in 1861, the row over *The Origin of Species* might have been much noisier had there not been a much greater row going on about *Essays and Reviews*.[1]

[1]   *Life and Letters of Dean Church,* ed. Mary C. Church (1894), 157.

Nevertheless, despite the hubbub, and despite the controversy which later in the decade raged over the publication by J. W. Colenso, Bishop of Natal, of his critical theory of the Pentateuch, the new views had come to stay, and the tide was running with the essayists. Benjamin Jowett, whose essay on 'The Interpretation of Scripture' was one of the most disturbing contributions to the volume, duly became the Master of Balliol (1870); Mark Pattison, whose penetrating study of eighteenth century English religious thought had excited little comment, became Rector of Lincoln College (1861), and Frederick Temple became Bishop of Exeter (1869), despite the strange alliance of the evangelical Lord Shaftesbury and the veteran Tractarian Dr Pusey, who formed a committee to resist his consecration. Temple's essay, indeed, had been harmless enough, but his ultimate translation to the Archbishopric of Canterbury in 1897 was sufficient proof that liberalism had triumphed in the Church.

The Tractarian movement by its very intransigence had provoked an inevitable reaction, and in Oxford the demand for freedom of thought and the right to employ critical methods of research, backed by such men as Jowett and Stanley, Mark Pattison, Froude and Matthew Arnold, could no longer be resisted. In 1871 religious tests were abolished and Dissenters were admitted to the University. An honour school of Jurisprudence and Modern History was established in 1853, and in 1872 Modern History was made a separate honour school. In 1870 an honour school of Historical Theology was established, in which the critical study of the Bible and Christian origins was taught. If the practice of studying the Bible and Christian doctrine merely 'historically', that is, undogmatically, seems to us today dull and inadequate, we must remember that, amidst the fierce denominational disputes of the closing years of the nineteenth century, it served a most useful purpose; it made it possible for Anglicans and Dissenters to study together and to discuss dispassionately all questions of the historical development of the Christian faith, and thus to get to know and to appreciate one another. The 'ecumenical' conception had not yet been born, and the half-way house of 'historical theology' —the undogmatic study of the Bible and Christian doctrine on the common basis of critical historical scholarship—was a necessary stage in its development. The quiet introduction of critical method into the newly founded honour school of Theology at Oxford and into the Theological Tripos at Cambridge[1] signalized the victory of liberalism in the Universities in the 'seventies; it was the outcome of a revolution in theological thinking more profound than any that had taken place in any previous century of the Church's history, not excluding the sixteenth. The traditional conception of the mode of divine revelation had been unobtrusively discarded, and this radical and far-reaching change had happened not as a development in dogmatic theology necessitated by changed philosophical attitudes, but as a direct consequence of the patient, determined and imperturbable devotion of Christian scholars engaged upon the quest for historical truth.

It was the characteristically empirical character of the

---

[1] The Theological Tripos at Cambridge was brought into existence by a decision of the Senate on 8 December, 1871, after years of discussion; at the same meeting the old Voluntary Theological Examination, established in 1842, was abolished. B. F. Westcott, then Regius Professor of Divinity, was influential in the founding of the Theological Tripos; in a circular letter which he addressed to the Bishops (16 September, 1871) he had expressed the hope that they would accept it as exempting successful candidates from the 'literary part' of the Ordination examination, 'that is, for a knowledge of the contents, the history, the external criticism of the Bible, the Prayer Book and the Articles (though not for their dogmatical interpretation)... It will be observed that ... special topics and dogmatics are left, as they must be, to the diocesan examinations.' See D. A. Winstanley, *Later Victorian Cambridge*, London, 1947, 161-3.

nineteenth century revolution in theology in England which made its course and its consequences so completely different from those of the development of theology on the Continent from Schleiermacher to Barth. In England the nineteenth century theological revolution did not begin with an *a priori* philosophical or dogmatic reconstruction, but with the recognition by scholars that the new critical and historical methods made far better sense (that is, 'history') of the Bible than did the old, unhistorical conception of a static, once-for-all, written revelation. The three greatest of them were Cambridge men, contemporaries and close friends, B. F. Westcott (1825-1901), J. B. Lightfoot (1828-89), and F. J. A. Hort (1828-92): Westcott succeeded Lightfoot as Bishop of Durham. Of the massive contribution of these three men to the scholarly understanding of Christian origins it is hardly necessary to speak;[1] it is probably true to say that they, more than any other three British theologians who could be named, guided the course of the theological revolution which was taking place in their days and shaped the future of theology in the Anglican Communion and perhaps in the English-speaking world. This they did not primarily as dogmatic theologians but as biblical and historical scholars; they did not put forward a new 'system' of theology or a new theory of revelation, though doubtless the latter was implied in their work. Their lasting contribution, apart from the weight of historical learning which they bequeathed to all future generations of scholars, was to show that the Church's ancient faith in Christ Incarnate, Crucified, Risen and Ascended, was in no way imperilled by the most scrupulous employment of critical historical methods but was rather established by it. The three greatest scholars of the century, employing the new methods, were men of deep Christian

[1] The celebrated critical edition of the Greek New Testament published in 1881 was the result of almost thirty years of close collaboration between Westcott and Hort.

faith, whole and unreduced. Some words written of Hort's life as a scholar and teacher by Bishop Westcott in 1893 apply equally to each of the three: 'A life so lived, however prolific in literary achievements, is more fruitful by what it is than by what it does . . . It confirms by a fresh testimony the belief in the unity of truth and being by which our ancient Universities are enabled to welcome and assimilate every increase of knowledge with untroubled joy.'[1] The Cambridge trio, we are reminded, even in the age of 'Darwinism', claimed all new knowledge as light from the God of truth who was revealed in Christ; while Hort was delivering his Hulsean Lectures—well worth reading today—he was also acting as examiner in the Natural Science Tripos examinations at Cambridge[2]. It has been truly said that 'the state of Divinity studies at Oxford (and, we may add, Cambridge) in the 'thirties and 'forties had been no sort of preparation for meeting the blizzard of intellectual doubt which blew across from Germany during the rest of the century';[3] yet by the end of the century the life and work of the Cambridge scholars had provided, as it were incidentally, the Anglican reply, confident and overwhelming, to the challenge of Strauss.

It thus becomes necessary to distinguish between two kinds of theological liberalism which had appeared on the English scene by the second half of the nineteenth century. First, there was the speculative or philosophical liberalism

---

[1] Prefatory Note to Hort's Hulsean Lectures, *The Way, the Truth, the Life* (1871), first published in 1893, xiv.

[2] Cf. Hort, *op. cit.*, 85: 'Christ's word, "I am the Truth,". . . speaks comfort and hope to all at any time who find themselves perplexed by the presence of truth not before known . . . It marks every truth which seems alien to Christ as a sign that the time is come for a better knowledge of Christ, since no truth can be alien to him who is the Truth.'

[3] B. A. Smith, *Dean Church: The Anglican Response to Newman*, London, 1958, 137.

of the 'Broad Churchmen' like Jowett or Stanley, whom R.W. Church described as 'a prophet and leader... but without a creed to preach':[1] it was willing to discard the 'dogmatic' and 'supernatural' elements in Christianity while hoping to conserve the traditional English respect for the moral teaching of Christ[2]. This kind of liberal thought, which has obvious affinities with continental Liberal Protestantism, survived well into the twentieth century and was represented by such 'modern churchmen' as Hastings Rashdall (1858-1924), W. R. Inge (1860-1954) and E. W. Barnes (1874-1953). But there was another, a second, type of liberal theological thought, which we will call liberal orthodoxy. It is represented pre-eminently by scholars like Westcott, Lightfoot and Hort, but, of course, there were many others. It included men whose background was Evangelical, like that of Lightfoot himself, and others, like R.W. Church, who became Dean of St Paul's in 1871, of the High Church tradition. Indeed, the declining years of those who had remained loyal to the conservatism of Pusey and the original Tractarians were saddened by the defection of the younger men; the publication of *Lux Mundi* in 1889, a volume of essays written by 'Anglo-Catholics', was indeed a sign of the times.

[1] B. A. Smith, *op. cit.*, 141.
[2] Two 'lives' of Christ appeared, which set what was to become the fashion of representing the 'historical' Jesus, as contrasted with the 'metaphysical Christ of the Creeds', as a nonsupernatural moral teacher: Sir John Seeley's *Ecce Homo* (1865), which at once brought fame to its originally anonymous author, and Dean F. W. Farrar's more restrained *Life of Christ* (1874), which went through twelve editions in a year. Matthew Arnold in *Literature and Dogma* (1873) was teaching that 'miracles do not happen' and that 'the human mind, as its experience widens, is turning away from them'; that God is no more than 'the enduring power, not ourselves, which makes for righteousness,' that 'religion is not simply morality, but morality touched by emotion'; and he defined righteousness as 'the method and secret and sweet reasonableness of Jesus'.

Its editor, Charles Gore (1853-1932, subsequently Bishop successively of Worcester, Birmingham and Oxford), had actually been appointed on Liddon's recommendation as the first Principal of Pusey House (1884), the institution in Oxford endowed by Pusey's friends for the preservation of his great library; yet it was Gore's essay in particular, on 'The Holy Spirit and Inspiration', which, restrained and innocuous as it seems to us today, nevertheless caused Liddon so much grief in the last year of his life. Though almost unreadable today, *Lux Mundi* is historically important because it marks the conversion of the intellectual leadership of the 'Anglo-Catholic' movement to the methods and ideals of historical criticism and to the point of view which we have called liberal orthodox; Gore and his friends carried over into the mainstream of Anglican life and thought that deep veneration of the Church's ancient tradition and continuity of doctrine which had characterized the attitude of Keble and Pusey and which proved so strong a bulwark against the inroads of speculative liberalism and creedless latitudinarianism. They also brought with them a sharp concern for social justice and an eager apologetic spirit, which sought to relate the age-long truth of Christian doctrine to the new knowledge which was being continuously brought forward not only by biblical and historical research, but also in science generally, and especially in the new-born sciences of sociology, anthropology and psychology. This interest is notably present in still another volume of essays, produced by a younger generation of the High Anglican tradition, *Essays Catholic and Critical* (1926), edited by E. G. Selwyn, lately Dean of Winchester. As its title suggests, the work is a defence of a genuinely liberal orthodoxy, and both of these words should be duly emphasized. As the editor remarked in the Preface to the first edition, 'the two terms Catholic and critical represent principles, habits and tempers of the religious mind which only reach their maturity in combination . . . there is no point at which they do not interact, and we are convinced that this interaction is necessary to any presentment of Christianity which is to claim the allegiance of the world today.'[1]

By the end of the nineteenth century there had emerged a restatement of the nature of the scriptural revelation such as had been necessitated by the rise of the new historical and critical methods. Perhaps its clearest expression is to be found in William Sanday's Bampton Lectures of 1893, published under the title *Inspiration* (1894), and delivered from that same pulpit of the University Church at Oxford from which but a few years earlier Pusey and Burgon and Liddon had so earnestly maintained the traditional view.[2] They embody the results of that long and painful process of rethinking which had been accomplished during the revolutionary half-century through which Sanday had then lived. He courageously faces and reverently answers the question which the historical scholarship of his generation had raised: if it is no longer possible to believe in the verbal inspiration and inerrancy of the Scriptures, in what sense ought a Christian to hold that the Bible is inspired and therefore authoritative? His answer to this question, which is the

---

[1] If the volume seems to us today somewhat 'dated', that is not merely because the various anthropological and psychological theories with which the essayists seek to reconcile the Christian faith are now largely superseded, but much more because the antidogmatic 'modernism' of the 'twenties, which they refuted, has quietly faded from the theological scene. It would seem that time itself has in a measure vindicated the claim of the editor in his Preface to the third edition (1929): 'It is because Catholicism is credal that it has been able to safeguard the worship of Christ in the modern world in a way which Liberal Protestantism does not.'

[2] Sanday (1843-1920) was successively Principal of Hatfield Hall, Durham, Dean Ireland's Professor of Exegesis and Lady Margaret Professor of Divinity at Oxford; his great commentary (with A. C. Headlam) on Romans (ICC) is a work of vast erudition and lasting value.

answer of the liberal orthodoxy of the later nineteenth and earlier twentieth centuries, is clear and precise, and it may be stated succinctly thus: it is not the words of the Bible that are inspired but the writers of the scriptural books. God's action is personal, not mechanical; he seeks to impart illumination to the minds of his servants, so that they think out the truth for themselves and make it their own. He is to be thought of as seeking to elicit the truth from his pupils, rather than as dictating to an amanuensis (or stenographer) words which the latter may or may not understand. Thus, the biblical revelation is a progressive revelation, being imparted gradually as the developing religious consciousness of mankind is able to receive it. What the scriptural writers have received from God is the experience of illumination, not a form of words; they have been inspired to understand more of the truth about God, but the words which they use to express this new understanding are their own. The new understanding which has arisen out of their experience of inspiration must necessarily clothe itself in the thought-forms and under the literary conventions of the writers' own day. The basic reality of revelation is thus the experience of God which the men of the Bible uniquely enjoyed, and their inspiration is demonstrated by their ability to convey the reality of this experience to subsequent generations of the human race. Thus, the 'errors' and infelicities of language which we find in the biblical writings are not to be ascribed to God; they are due to the inevitable limitations of men who lived in particular historical phases of the gradual unfolding of the divine truth. We are therefore allowed—indeed, compelled—in the light of the later, developed revelation of the true character of God to believe that the biblical writers were mistaken in thinking that God had commanded the slaughter of the women and children of the Amalekites (I Sam. 15.3) or that he had enjoined the execution of witches (Ex. 22.18). What we have in the Bible is the record of God's progressive revelation of himself, as men were able to understand it, from the days of primitive animism or tribal nationalism to those of the lofty monotheism and universalism of the later prophets and of the New Testament. The Bible is the story of the divine education of the human race, and as such is our uniquely valuable and indispensable authority and guide in the apprehension of religious truth.

In three ways especially this theory of biblical inspiration perfectly enshrined the characteristic presuppositions of the nineteenth century mind. In the first place, it is thoroughly evolutionary. So far from being opposed to the ruling scientific concept of evolution, the Bible was a remarkable illustration of it; it records the evolution of men's ideas about God from their crude beginnings to their noblest expression in the life and teaching of Jesus Christ. Darwin had told the story of man's biological evolution; theological scholarship could now complete the story by telling of the moral and spiritual evolution of the human race. Instead of a static, undeveloping revelation, there was now room for real change and for historical progress in the idea of revelation itself. The whole story of man's development from its sub-human origins could now be viewed as progress towards that

> '. . . one far-off divine event
> To which the whole creation moves.'[1]

Secondly, Sanday's conception of inspiration was able to make full use of the category of 'religious experience', which the nineteenth century had inherited from the Romantic Movement. The task of the literary and historical criticism of the Bible was to analyse and set forth the evidence which the scriptural writers themselves present to us concerning the nature and content of their experience of inspiration, or

---

[1]   Tennyson, *In Memoriam,* Conclusion, st. xxxvi.

of their awareness of God. When this task is performed, the normative quality of the religious experience of the men of the Bible is clearly perceived, and we come to understand something of how it is that the Bible can awaken in us the consciousness of the divine which the prophets and apostles so richly enjoyed. The *locus* of revelation was thus removed from the cold propositional truths of a written document to the warm and living experience of real men and women, who were just as 'human' and alive as we are today, who shared the same hopes and fears, joys and griefs, emotions and intuitions as we do, and who can therefore help and guide us in our efforts to solve our human problems. The historical approach to the Bible had made the biblical characters 'come alive' as real people, whose 'inspiration' lay in the fact that they were able to communicate their own deep and normative experience of God to every subsequent generation.

Thirdly, Sanday regarded the new method of approach to the Bible as essentially inductive and therefore in accord with the scientific temper and method of the modern age. The nineteenth century revolution in theological method meant that theology was now no longer a deductive science, deducing necessary conclusions from inerrant propositions written in the Scriptures. Before the rise of the method of modern historical science, it had been held that the task of the theologian was to deduce true conclusions from the infallible words of the Bible, and then to arrange them in an orderly system ('systematic theology') which could be regarded as itself the sufficient summary of the divine revelation ('revealed theology'). Peter Lombard in his *Sentences,* Thomas Aquinas in his *Summa,* Calvin in his *Institutes* and Pearson in his *Exposition of the Creed* (1659), all believed that they were doing precisely that. But now, after the 'Copernican' revolution in theological method of the nineteenth century, theology, if she still remained 'Queen of the

Sciences', abdicated from her absolute, deductive throne, and attempted to become a strictly constitutional monarch, employing the same empirical methods as her sister sciences. Theology in the view of Sanday and his friends was properly an inductive science, reaching its provisional conclusions as the result of a wide and scientific induction from the evidence of man's religious consciousness as it was presented most clearly and compellingly in the biblical and Christian history. Starting from the normative expression of the religious experience of mankind as found in the Bible, it infers from the evidence that the scriptural writers were directed by a 'larger Mind', or that behind the individual biblical books there lay 'a central Intelligence' which alone can account for their astonishing unity and consistent development over a period of a thousand kaleidoscopic years. By no other hypothesis can we account for the astonishing unity of outlook which the biblical literature displays. This argument for the inspiration of Scripture, as thus re-stated by Sanday upon an inductive basis, is a very old one in the history of Christian thought. It had, indeed, in its traditional form, been the principal argument for the inspiration of the Bible adduced by H. P. Liddon, the Bampton Lecturer of 1866. Liddon had argued that beneath all the wide divergences of the various scriptural books there underlies and informs them such a manifest 'unity of drift and purpose' as to imply 'the continuous action of a Single Mind'. There is no parallel in any other language to this strange phenomenon: the whole literature of a nation for over a thousand years bears the imprint of 'one Infallible Intelligence', slowly working out the rich organic harmony of a single, developing theme. We are compelled to speak not only about the books, but about the Book ('Bible'), not only about the diversity of the parts but about the unity of the whole. Christian insight down the ages has been led to acknowledge 'the fundamental unity of all Revelation, underlying and strictly compatible with its superficial variety'. One part of Scripture illuminates another, even though removed from it by centuries of time; the later lies concealed in the earlier; the Gospel is shewn beforehand to Abraham; the Law and the Prophets are fulfilled in the Gospel. The history and literature of no other people can be read in this way; in Greek or English, for example, 'it would be absurd to appeal to a primitive annalist or poet with a view to determining the meaning of an author of some later age . . . We do not expect to find in Chaucer or in Clarendon a clue to or a forecast of the true sense of Macaulay or of Tennyson. No one has ever imagined that either the Greek or the English literature is a whole in such sense that any common purpose runs persistently throughout it, or that we can presume upon the existence of a common responsibility to some one line of thought in the several authors who have created it, or that each portion is under any kind of obligation to be in some profound moral and intellectual conformity with the rest.'[1] But the Bible, the entire literature of the Hebrew people from Moses to the Apostles, is just such a unity, and we are therefore compelled to attribute its inspiration to the work of the Eternal Spirit of God.

This argument for scriptural inspiration, which is almost as old as Christianity itself, is still powerful and impressive.[2] What Sanday did was to shew that it can be re-stated in terms of his new 'inductive' view without losing anything of its compelling force. Indeed he claimed that the new historical and critical methods actually strengthened it, because they shewed that it could be grounded upon a genuinely scientific induction from the evidence. The fact of divine revelation through the Scriptures was thus no longer a matter

---

[1] *The Divinity of our Lord and Saviour Jesus Christ,* Bampton Lectures of 1866, ii (13th ed., 1889, 47).
[2] Cf. G. A. F. Knight, *A Christian Theology of the Old Testament* (1959), 155, 160. See also Chapter 8 below.

of mere dogmatic assertion or of unsupported speculation, but could be shewn to be susceptible of empirical verification as a result of the most rigorous application of critical scientific method. In relation to the dominant liberal ideology of the late nineteenth and earlier twentieth centuries Sanday's re-statement constituted a valuable piece of apologetic, and his work illustrates the truth that the task of the apologist is always that of re-presenting the ancient truth under the new forms of contemporary understanding. If the nineteenth century forms seem to us no longer 'contemporary', that is no criticism of Sanday, and his example reminds us of our duty in a later age to present the great truth of the unity of the Scriptures to our own generation in such a way that our contemporaries will be predisposed to draw the right and indeed the inevitable conclusions from it. Sanday and his friends had done their work well, and their influence was considerable in the first quarter of the twentieth century; they saved many thoughtful people, who had encountered the full force of the shock of the new approach to the Bible, from lapsing into scepticism or at best into speculative liberalism of the Matthew Arnold type, by shewing how a lively faith in the inspiration of Scripture could be supported by the principles of historical and literary criticism. The Anglican 'Liberal Evangelical' movement, led by V. F. Storr and others, and also the liberal orthodoxy which Bishop Gore and his friends represented, were fortified in the conviction that the acceptance of the new critical standpoint need not imply any reduction of the full Catholic faith in the person and work of Christ as the Church's ancient Creeds had affirmed it.

But, of course, Sanday's position, precisely because it was so persuasively set forth in the thought-forms of his own day, is not a final resting-place for us today. It belongs essentially to that period of thought which was ushered in by the Romantic Movement and which set such high store upon man and his 'experience'. Its weakness, as with so much Christian apologetics, is that it goes so far in the direction of the new, non-biblical categories (such as that of 'religious experience') that it tends to obscure important aspects of enduring biblical truth. Hence, when in the course of time these 'modern' categories themselves begin to lose their compelling vigour and men are turning to new ones, the faith, which has now been identified with the old ones, seems to many to be itself old-fashioned and moribund. Today the category of religious experience does not seem adequate, as it formerly did, to the task of explaining the authority of the biblical revelation.[1] If we know that the Bible is inspired because it is 'inspiring', we are left with nothing to say to anyone who claims that he finds other religious literature equally 'inspiring'. And what shall we say of those parts of Scripture which we do not find 'inspiring', for instance, parts of Leviticus or Zephaniah? Ought we not to make a new anthology of religious passages which the modern mind really does find 'inspiring', drawing not only from the Hebrew and Christian Scriptures, but also from St Augustine and Thomas à Kempis, Luther, Bunyan and Wesley, William Temple and C. S. Lewis? And why should we not include in it inspiring passages from outside the Christian tradition altogether—from Plato, Marcus Aurelius, Confucius and the sacred writings of the East? Or, in other words, why have a Bible at all? And why, if revelation is progressive, should the revelation have stopped about the end of the first century, or the beginning of the second century A.D., when the latest books of the New Testament were written? Ought we not to expect progress in the know-

---

[1] This is not to deprecate the importance of the argument from religious experience in the sphere of apologetics or the philosophy of religion; it is still a very strong 'argument' in the traditional sense. See H. D. Lewis, *Our Experience of God* (London, 1959).

ledge of God to continue with the developing capacities of the evolving human race? It has become clearer today that the authority of the Bible, as Christians have traditionally understood it, cannot be explained by means of the highly subjective categories of 'inspiration' and 'religious experience'. Any such explanation makes man and his experience the criterion of divine truth, and therefore does not explain the mysterious phenomenon with which the Bible confronts us, namely, a divine authority which we do not judge but which on the contrary searches and judges us. To attempt to find the explanation of the phenomenon of biblical authority in the sphere of 'inspiration' is to seek for understanding in a place where the Bible itself does not look for it. The attempt to 'explain' the Bible in non-biblical categories is bound to fail, and such efforts have given rise in the past to most of the classical misinterpretations of biblical truth which have disturbed the life of the Church. The very word 'inspiration' is hardly a biblical word at all. In the New Testament it occurs only in the Authorized Version (KJV) translation of II Tim. 3.16, where the Greek text suggests that God has breathed into the 'dead' words of the Old Testament Scriptures the breath of life, as once he breathed into man's nostrils and man became a living soul.[1] The AV translation ('All Scripture is given by inspiration of God . . .') has behind it a long history of misinterpretation, since Alexandrian and pagan notions of inspiration as a kind of divine *afflatus* had entered the Church as early as the days of Justin Martyr in the middle of the second century.[2] From these misconceptions the rise of modern historical criticism in the nineteenth century has set us free. But what the nine-

---

[1] The RV translation runs, 'Every Scripture inspired *(theopneustos)* of God is also profitable . . .' The reference is to Gen. 2.7 (cf. Wisdom 15.11; also II Cor. 3.14-17).

[2] For a brief account of the matter see Alan Richardson, *Christian Apologetics*, 202-5; for a fuller study see R. P. C. Hanson, *Allegory and Event* (1959), especially Chap. 7.

teenth century had not yet realized, if Sanday's work may be taken as its culminating point, was that the non-biblical category of inspiration, whether in its ancient Alexandrian or in its modern Romantic form, cannot provide a satisfactory basis for the re-statement of the truth concerning the authority of the Bible in the age of science.

4

FROM SCHLEIERMACHER TO BARTH

OUGHT we to agree with the view expressed, for instance, by the late Professor H. R. Mackintosh that the nineteenth century was the greatest century in Christian theology since the fourth? Mark Pattison regarded the period of the rise of the new historical methods at the beginning of the century in Germany as the fourth great period of doctrinal development in Christian history, the others being the fourth century, the thirteenth century and the Reformation period.[1] We may, perhaps, agree with such a verdict, provided that we think in terms of theological method rather than of theological conclusions. The nineteenth century settled nothing; it raised a number of important questions, but its answers to them satisfy no one in the twentieth century. Even in the restricted sphere of biblical criticism some of the 'assured results' of nineteenth century investigation—the Graf-Wellhausen hypothesis, for example, or the existence of Q[2]—have been called in question in recent years; while in the dogmatic sphere the general trend of nineteenth century liberal theology has been completely reversed by the rise of the 'dialectical' theology of Barth and Brunner. Looked at from the aspect of its 'conclusions' the nineteenth century might seem to have contributed little of permanent signifi-

---

[1] *Essays,* II, 150f.
[2] See, for instance, E. Nielsen, *Oral Tradition* (London, 1954); J. Bright, *Early Israel in Recent History Writing* (London 1956); A. M. Farrer, 'On Dispensing with Q', in *Studies in the Gospels,* ed. D. E. Nineham (Oxford, 1955).

cance to the development of theology; but such an inference could be based only upon a mistaken notion of what theology is. The significance of scientific investigation does not lie in its conclusions, regarded as 'assured results'; 'conclusions' are always subject to revision and correction. The only permanent thing about science is its method: the glory of modern science lies not in its results, impressive though these are, but in its method. It is not otherwise with theology. The nineteenth century is of permanent importance in the development of theology, not because of any conclusions which it established, but because it essayed the first tentative employment of a new theological method. The new method which it devised was indeed far from perfect, and the development of an adequate theological methodology remains still the most pressing task confronting theologians in the twentieth century. If the first results of the use of the new critical methods in the nineteenth century seem to us today meagre and disappointing, that is because we no longer share the distinctively nineteenth century presuppositions; it does not mean that we reject the critical methods themselves. Faced by the rise of the new historical knowledge, to which they had themselves so notably contributed, the theologians of the nineteenth century were obliged to discard the traditional theological method of systematizing the inerrant propositions of an infallible written revelation and to devise and employ a new method by which theological truth could be articulated and defended.

The theologian who dominates the nineteenth century on the continent of Europe is F.D.E. Schleiermacher (1768-1834). Karl Barth applies to him some words which he himself had used of Frederick the Great: 'He did not found a school, but an era.'[1] After a narrowly pietistic upbringing amongst the Moravians, he encountered the rationalism of

[1] *From Rousseau to Ritschl* (London, 1959), 306.

the Enlightenment in the University of Halle (1787); but it was after his appointment as a hospital preacher in Berlin (1796) that he came under the influence of Friedrich von Schlegel (1772-1829) and other leaders of the Romantic Movement. It was from Romanticism that he derived not only the most original but also the most questionable elements in his theology. From Schlegel he learnt not to be afraid of science, more particularly historical investigation. Impartial historical criticism would deliver theology from the tedious polemics of the rationalists and the supernaturalists alike. 'Schleiermacher, with that intuitiveness which genius gives, understands the revolution which this renovation of science will necessarily effect in theology. Criticism [as practised by the rationalists] has been till now the enemy of Christianity; it has taken pleasure in unveiling her weaknesses, in sneering at her miracles and her dogmas; but in the future it will be the guardian of the sanctuary, the most faithful and the most valiant auxiliary of the faith'.[1] The use of the word 'genius' in this quotation is hardly too strong, if we have regard to the destructive use which was made of biblical criticism by the eighteenth century rationalists or by sceptical contemporaries of Schleiermacher, such as H.E.G. Paulus (1761-1851). Schleiermacher's enthusiastic and unqualified acceptance of the principle of historical criticism marks a turning point of crucial importance in the development of Christian theology. It is scarcely too much to say that it initiated on the continent of Europe the revolution in theology which makes the nineteenth century no less important in the history of Christian thought than the fourth, the thirteenth or the sixteenth. In Schleiermacher's day biblical criticism was still only at a very rudimentary and immature stage of its development; and it is hardly surprising that the great majority of thoughtful Christians were unable to con-

[1] F. Lichtenberger, *History of German Theology in the Nineteenth Century* (Edinburgh, 1889), 56.

ceive of its becoming an auxiliary of the faith.[1] Schleiermacher himself was not outstanding as a biblical critic, and his own critical position is by later standards naïve and unscientific. He regards St John's Gospel as the historically reliable source of our knowledge of the life and teaching of Jesus, since it was written by one of his intimate disciples; the Synoptic Gospels are further removed in time and in understanding from their subject. As we have said, it is not the conclusions but the method which is the significant matter; it is Schleiermacher's acceptance of historical criticism, rather than his actual use of it, which makes him so important in the development of modern theology.

The acceptance of a critical attitude towards the Bible meant that Schleiermacher had to formulate a new doctrine of revelation, since now for him revelation could no longer be found in the infallible words of Scripture. This he did by

[1] In England in the 1820s and '30s German theology in general was regarded as dangerously blasphemous, because of the sceptical tendencies of the biblical critics. Connop Thirlwall (1797-1875), later Bishop of St David's, ventured before taking Holy Orders to translate Schleiermacher's Essay on Luke, though he published it anonymously (1825); he remarked that 'it would almost seem as if in Oxford the knowledge of German subjected a divine to the same suspicion of heterodoxy which we know was attached some centuries back to the knowledge of Greek.' (It was a pity that Thirlwall did not translate one of Schleiermacher's more important works, for the *Kritischer Versuch über die Schriften des Lukas* (1821) is a not very successful attempt to prove that Luke's Gospel is a composite work.) In the same year (1825) Hugh James Rose was delivering his abusive and ill-informed sermons, *The State of Protestantism in Germany Described,* from the University pulpit in Cambridge; he seems hardly even to have heard of Schleiermacher. German scholars were understandably aggrieved by such wilful misrepresentations, and even Dr Pusey was moved to correct Rose's distortions (see the work mentioned on p. 59 above); Rose accused Pusey of 'liberalizing'! Schleiermacher's theology was little noticed in England until the second half of the century: as we have already observed, the revolution in theology in England received little direct stimulus from Germany but pursued its own insular course.

means of two key concepts. The first is his conception of Christianity as a positive historical religion. Thus, he parts company with the rationalists and deists of the eighteenth century, who looked for a universal religion of reason, valid for all men in all lands irrespective of their particular historical situation. Christianity is not a universal religion, 'the religion of reason' as such. Like other religions, it is a particular religion which began at a certain moment of history and thereafter developed in a particular historical movement and exists today in the consciousness of particular groups of real men and women. It is indeed the highest form of religion, having room within it for all that is true and valuable in other religions; but it is nevertheless, like them, a particular stream of religious consciousness in the history of mankind. This is what is meant by a 'positive historical religion.' It cannot be conceived apart from its history; that is to say, it cannot be separated, even in thought, from its Founder or from the Church. Schleiermacher's view is through-and-through Christological. Christ introduced a new element into the developing consciousness of humanity, namely, a new consciousness of God, a complete dependence upon and union with the will of God. What was but imperfectly realised in even the most devout of men was wholly and perfectly realised in Christ, who is thus the ideal type of man, the final expression of all that the human race may and indeed must become. There is a perfect union of the divine nature and of human nature in Christ's person, from which his absolute holiness proceeds; the appearance of such a God-consciousness, of such an existence of God in human life, is itself the miracle of miracles. It needs no attestation by the alleged miracles of the Gospels, even by the resurrection; it is attested by the continuation in history of this same God-consciousness, that is, by the experience of the Christian Church. The historical Church is divided into various confessions, but each of them preserves some valid aspect of this rich and many-sided awareness of God. The dogmas which the churches proclaim are but their inadequate attempts to articulate the God-consciousness which they possess; though they profess to be statements of absolute truth, they are in reality only descriptive or psychological expressions of the corporate religious awareness of particular groups of believers at particular times. Those doctrines which are primary deliverances of the religious consciousness, such as those of the Incarnation or the Exaltation of Christ to the right hand of God, are of permanent significance and value; those which we do not find attested by our religious awareness, such as the doctrines of the preexistence of Christ or of the Trinity, are not to be taken seriously; indeed, Schleiermacher deals with the doctrine of the Trinity only in an appendix to his chief dogmatic treatise.[1] The work of Christ, which Schleiermacher speaks of as 'liberation' or 'redemption', is the reconciliation of the supernatural and the natural, or the establishment of the Kingdom of God, that is, the complete renovation and integration of man's moral and social life by the spiritual fellowship of the Church, the whole body of believers who are animated by the Spirit of Christ. Christ is the archetypal image of humanity, and still today has the power to transform individual believers so that they together become the firstfruits of that Kingdom which he came to found.

The second key-concept of Schleiermacher's thought has already been mentioned several times in our exposition of the first, and indeed the two are quite inseparable. It is the concept of the religious consciousness. Doubtless it owes something to the warm personal devotion of the Moravians, experienced during Schleiermacher's adolescence; but it

[1] *Der Christliche Glaube nach den Grundsätzen der evangelischen Kirche im Zusammenhange dargestellt* (1821; 2nd ed., 1830-1); English translation, *The Christian Faith*, by H. R. Mackintosh and J. S. Stewart, Edinburgh, 1928.

owes more to the Romantic cult of personal feeling in its strong reaction from the cold rationalism of the Enlightenment. Already in the work of his youth, the *Reden* (1799)[1], he had in the second discourse *(Über das Wesen der Religion)* defined religion neither as knowledge nor as activity, but as a feeling, an intuition: 'a sense and taste for the infinite'. Dogmas are only secondary or derivative elements in religion, which is essentially the revelation of the Infinite within the sanctuary of the individual soul; the cultured despiser of religion is despising his own deepest aspirations. Religion by being itself man's quest for the Infinite is in reality the source of all human scientific, cultural, moral and social endeavour. The individual's estrangement from Humanity is overcome by his union with Archetypal Humanity, God in Christ, who leads mankind into all truth. The New Testament is normative of the human experience of God in Christ, because the first generation of Christians drank the pure water near its source; but it does not contain within it the mighty flood of God-consciousness which future ages would bring forth. Other books may become 'Bible' for us as we move forward to the day when, through the religious consciousness which Christ has imparted to mankind, redeemed humanity shall no longer have need of a Mediator and the archetypal image shall be realised in the whole race. Thus Schleiermacher, who was equally at home translating Plato with Schlegel or in the Academy of the Sciences as in the pulpit or lecture-room, sought to draw all life and all human endeavour into that stream of religious awareness which had its origin in the historical Jesus and which one day would bring to fruition the aspirations of the whole human race. Man's awareness of dependence upon God, and

---

[1] *Über die Religion. Reden an die Gebildeten unter ihren Verächtern*; English translation, *On Religion: Speeches to its Cultured Despisers*, by J. Oman, 1893; new edition, New York and London, 1958.

therefore of the connection of all his life with God, and so finally his complete union with God, is the subject of theology; and thus Schleiermacher's theology becomes a theology of feeling, or, more precisely, a theology of the religious consciousness.

Schleiermacher's influence throughout the nineteenth century in Europe can hardly be exaggerated; every theologian found it necessary to define his own position in relation to him. The two main theses of Schleiermacher's theology became the framework, as it were, of the characteristic theological outlook of the century, which is generally styled Liberal Protestantism. Liberal theology in the continental sense was controlled by the two guiding principles which Schleiermacher had first clearly articulated: Christianity is a 'positive' (not a universal-rational) religion, similar in kind though doubtless superior to other positive religions; and the *locus* of revelation is in man's religious consciousness. This framework allowed ample room for the development of the science of biblical criticism, since it did not fetter the latter by any restricting dogmatic presuppositions established in advance of the enquiry. Or, more accurately, new and experimental presuppositions could be tested, for it is not possible to engage in presuppositionless historical construction. Thus, the Tübingen School, founded by F. C. Baur (1792-1860), who began as a disciple of Schleiermacher, endeavoured to interpret the New Testament by means of Hegel's dialectical conception of history: the 'thesis' of the original Jewish Christianity (the 'Petrinists') was contested by the 'antithesis' of Gentile Christianity (the 'Paulinists') and the conflict was finally resolved by the emergence of Catholicism, the 'synthesis', in the second century. This hypothesis involved the rejection of the Pauline authorship of many of St Paul's Epistles (of all except Galatians, I and II Corinthians and Romans) and the dating of the Gospels well into the second century. Traditionally orthodox Christians were deeply shocked, but such suggestions were not out of place within the two-concept framework of Liberal Protestantism. It was a matter of merely academic interest *how* the stream of Christian religious consciousness had begun; the important matters were the deliverances of the religious consciousness itself. After the hey-day of the Tübingen School had passed away with the 'forties, a more soberly scientific study of the evidence soon demonstrated the inadequacy of the Hegelian hypothesis to explain the historical data of the New Testament and of early Christian literature; criticism settled down to the more pedestrian task of examining the evidence in the light of the many other less extravagant hypotheses which were available, and the main outlines of a generally accepted critical position came into view.

The outstanding theologian of the second half of the nineteenth century, Albrecht Ritschl (1822-89), had studied under Baur, and in his early works he defended the Tübingen thesis; but in the second edition (1857) of his *Die Entstehung der altkatholischen Kirche* (1850) he entirely repudiated it. As with all the members of the dominant 'Ritschlian School' (Kaftan, Herrmann, Kattenbusch, Loofs, Harnack, Troeltsch, etc.), the theology of Ritschl rested comfortably within the Liberal Protestant two-concept framework. Indeed, Ritschl pushed the notion of the supreme value of the religious consciousness to its extreme limit. He rejected all metaphysics as decisively as the Logical Positivists of the nineteenthirties were subsequently to do; like them he failed to notice that the 'rejection' of metaphysics could be accomplished only within the framework of a metaphysical view. Unlike them, however, he rejected metaphysics in the interests of pure religion. Religion is a form of human experience which cannot be reduced to any other form of it. The deliverances of the religious consciousness are judgments of value, not judgments of existence; when the Church affirms that Jesus is divine, what is being said is that Jesus has for us the value of God; no metaphysical statement is implied. The metaphysics of the Chalcedonian doctrine of 'substance' and 'natures' or of the speculative rationalism of Hegelian idealism is an alien intrusion into Christian thought. Ritschl and his School are equally distrustful of mysticism. The right relationship to God is that of faith, which is made possible by the individual's joyful recognition of the justification which Christ's life and death have achieved for us; but it is only through the Church, the fellowship of true believers, that justification or the forgiveness of sins and liberation into new life are possible for individuals. Christianity is a positive, historical faith, inseparable from its historical Founder, and its end is the Kingdom of God, the moral integration of humanity in the great, divine fellowship of love. In this teaching Ritschl believed that he was recalling theology to the pure first principles not only of Luther but also of the New Testament itself, a faith uncorrupted by philosophical or scholastic speculation, and independent of any theory of scriptural inspiration. Scripture is the sole rule and norm of faith, because through it alone we are brought into contact with the faith of the earliest Christian community in its unsullied freshness.[1]

It is impossible in a brief account to do justice to the richness and variety of German theology in the nineteenth century; nothing more has been attempted here than to describe the main features of the dominant theological outlook, that of 'Liberal Protestantism'. In the next chapter something more will be said about the historical criticism of the Gospels and the place which was given to the 'Jesus of history' in the thought of the period. The century that began with the new

---

[1]   Ritschl's most important work, *Die christliche Lehre von der Rechtfertigung und Versöhnung,* was published in 3 vols., 1870-4, of which there are English translations of Vol. I by J. S. Black (1872) and of Vol. III, ed. by H. R. Mackintosh and A. B. Macaulay (Edinburgh, 1900). See also A. E. Garvie, *The Ritschlian Theology* (1899); J. K. Mozley, *Ritschlianism* (1909).

method adumbrated in Schleiermacher's *Reden,* which went through six editions during the lifetime of the author, closed with the publication of a small work by the immensely learned historian of doctrine, Adolf von Harnack (1851-1930), *Das Wesen des Christentums* (1900),[1] which was widely influential during the first decade of the twentieth century. In Harnack's view Christianity was still a 'positive historical religion'; it was in fact 'the religion of Jesus', which consisted essentially in two affirmations, the Fatherhood of God and the Brotherhood of Man. Since Jesus himself did not believe that he was the Son of God, the natural conclusion was that we need not believe in it either. The metaphysics about Christ's divine 'nature' which culminated in the Definition of Chalcedon was the unfortunate result of the Hellenization of the simple, original Galilean Gospel. Thus, the earliest 'Christianity' was essentially a theology without a Christology; and so we reach the classic Liberal Protestant distinction between the pure 'religion of Jesus' and the 'religion about Jesus' with which St Paul and the Hellenizers quickly obscured it. This is the final and logical working out of the presuppositions of Schleiermacher and his successors; Harnack 'remained fundamentally Ritschlian to the last.'[2] Karl Barth, who studied under Harnack, speaks of the year 1900 as marking the climax of nineteenth century theology and says that Harnack's book was responsible for a renaissance of Schleiermacher around 1910.[3] Elsewhere

1 English translation, *What is Christianity?* (1931), recently re-issued in paper backs by Harpers (New York; Hamish Hamilton, London, 1958). It was this work which provoked Loisy's reply, *L'Évangile et l'Église* (1908). See A. R. Vidler, *The Modernist Movement in the Roman Church* (Cambridge, 1934), 111.
2 J. M. Creed, *The Divinity of Jesus Christ* (Cambridge, 1938), 101.
3 In 'Evangelical theology in the nineteenth century'. Page 57 in *God, Grace and Gospel* (Scottish Journal of Theology Occasional Papers no. 8), Edinburgh, 1959; this is a translation of three small works by Barth. Its American edition is entitled *The Humanity of God* (John Knox Press, 1960).

he says that Schleiermacher was studied and honoured more in 1910 than in 1830, when he was still overshadowed by Hegel.[1] But the renaissance was shortlived; 'the century of Schleiermacher' came to an end in 1914. The Age of Progress, ushered in by Herder and the Romantics, perished in the convulsions of the First World War. Like so many other nineteenth century aspirations, Liberal Protestant theology did not survive the cataclysm, although, as we shall see, it left behind it many traces and influences which are still active today.

Karl Barth, who more than any other single figure has dominated the European theological scene since 1919, when Der Römerbrief[2] appeared, has told us of the event which first made him realise that he must break away from the whole theology and outlook of his revered Liberal Protestant teachers: it was the discovery one day in August, 1914, that almost all of them had signed a declaration issued by ninety-three German intellectuals supporting the war policy of Kaiser Wilhelm II. 'At least for me the theology of the nineteenth century had no future.'[3] It would seem that Barth's reaction was that, if 'the deliverances of the religious consciousness' led to results as strange as this, then the assumption that the interrogation of man's religious consciousness is the proper theological method of discovering truth must be decisively renounced. The truth is not to be found in man's subjective awareness, his 'feelings' or even in his conscience, for man is a fallen creature and the truth is not in him. Theological truth must be the truth which man does not possess in himself; it comes to him from beyond or 'above' himself, vertically; it is the truth from which, save by the mercy of God in his revelation in Christ, man is alienated by

---

[1] *From Rousseau to Ritschl*, 306f.
[2] English translation by E. C. Hoskyns, *The Epistle to the Romans*, Oxford, 1932.
[3] *God, Grace and Gospel*, 58. 'Evangelical theology in the nineteenth century' is an address delivered in 1957.

his sin. Schleiermacher's rousing sermons on behalf of the Prussian war effort against Napoleon, or Harnack's defence of the Kaiser, can be justified only by a theology which has become anthropology and which can therefore identify patriotic men's crazy idealism with the will of God. In the crisis of 1914–18, as later in the struggle of the Confessing Church against the crooked cross of the Nazis and the 'German Christians', Barth arose to speak an authentic word from God, a prophet to whom amidst the shaking of the nations the Word of the Lord had come. This is his greatness. In this way the Swiss country pastor at Safenwil (1911-21) became a theologian. The famous Professor—first at Göttingen (1921), then at Münster (1925), then at Bonn (1930), and lastly, after he had been deprived of his chair at Bonn by the Nazis, at Basel (1935), the author of the massive *Die Kirchliche Dogmatik* (1932, continuing)—is the prophet who (in his own metaphor) 'rang the bell' in his *Römerbrief* in 1919 and caught the attention of a disillusioned generation, which no longer looked upon the world through the rose-tinted spectacles of Romantic Liberalism.

The new standpoint of which Barth is the outstanding representative and which replaced Liberal Protestantism as the dominant European theological outlook in the post-war world is often spoken of as 'the Dialectical Theology'.[1] It is so called because it rejects the scholastic (Catholic or Protestant) view which regards God as an 'object' of theological reasoning (*via positiva*) and also the mystical notion that only what God is *not* is capable of being thought (*via negativa*), transcending the 'yes' and 'no' of these methods by means of a third approach (*via dialectica*), which affirms that God is known, neither as object nor yet merely negatively,

[1] Amongst the members of this 'school', although they do not necessarily regard Barth (b. 1886)) as their founder or leader, are usually reckoned F. Gogarten (b. 1887), E. Thurneysen (b. 1888) and E. Brunner (b. 1889). They have in common the 'dialectical' approach, despite Barth's later qualifications.

but as Subject, as the 'Thou' who mysteriously and miraculously reveals himself to men in his own unconditioned freedom. Two very important consequences follow from this dialectical approach. First, because God is Subject and can never be made the object of our thinking, like the 'things' in the created world which natural science (including psychology) can investigate 'objectively', our knowledge of God cannot be written down in a series of propositions, which can then be set up as 'the truth about God,' whether in the Scriptures, or in the Creeds, or in systems of dogmatic theology. God is known to us only in personal encounter, that is, in and through the Word which he has addressed to us in Jesus Christ. There is no other knowledge of God, whether by 'natural theology' or philosophy or mystical 'experience' or anything else; Christ is the sole means of the knowledge of God: 'No one knoweth the Father save the Son, and he to whomsoever the Son willeth to reveal him' (Matt. 11.27; Luke 10.22). In this conception of the nature of the knowledge of God the influence of Kierkegaard's existentialism is clearly seen; the very word 'dialectical' in this context is derived from Kierkegaard. The second consequence of the dialectical approach follows inevitably: nothing can be discovered about God by means of the analysis of our human religious consciousness. Psychology may properly investigate religious 'experience', but psychology is not therefore in a better position than zoology or microbiology to tell us anything about God.[1] There can be no natural theology based

---

[1] In the English-speaking world the Ritschlian influence probably was at its zenith during the nineteen-twenties, though it was never strong in England itself. Consider the following passage from a book first published in New York in 1930: 'What is most needed ... is a new natural theology, not beginning with nature but with religious experience, not rationalistic but empirical in method ... This new empirical theology is already in the making. Among the books which have contributed to its making, I would name Hocking's *Meaning of God in Human Experience*, Professor

on psychology; religious experience is not a biblical category of explanation, nor can it have any role in dogmatics.

Thus, these two consequences of the dialectical method involve the complete rejection of the two guiding principles of Schleiermacher's theological method, which, as we saw, became the framework of nineteenth century Liberal Protestantism. Christianity is not 'a positive historical religion', like other religions, and theology is not a special branch of the wider study of the history of religion. 'Christianity' is strictly not 'religion' at all: it is the divine revelation of truth and as such is not comparable with 'the religions' of the world. Its scientific study is properly dogmatics, and dogmatics must necessarily be *Church* dogmatics, for only amongst those who receive the revelation of God by faith can the truth be known. The truth is God's revelation in Christ, and therefore dogmatics is essentially Christology. Theology is concerned not with the deliverances of the religious consciousness but with faith in Jesus Christ; and faith, which is miraculously created in man by the free and unconditioned operation of the Holy Spirit of God, is not to be subsumed under the general category of religious experience, for it has nothing in common with it. Indeed, the religious idealism even of 'good' men must be annihilated before they can come to faith, and therefore apologetics is no part of the theologian's proper task. Religious experience and faith in Christ are discontinuous, and men cannot be led by apologetic arguments from the one to the other. The apologist has

Lyman's *Experience of God in Modern Life,* Professor Macintosh's *Theology as an Empirical Science,* and Professor Wieman's much-discussed writings. Common to all these thinkers is the tendency to regard God, provisionally at least, not as a Being behind and apart from the world of human experience, but rather as a Being revealed *in* human experience, a Dependable Factor in it which can be isolated by scientific analysis just as one isolates chemical elements or bacteria or vitamines' (Walter Marshall Horton, *Theism and the Modern Mood,* London, 1931, 70f.).

ceased to be a theologian and has turned himself into a philosopher; he goes out to meet the unbeliever carrying a white flag.[1] Similarly the world of culture, of science and progress, is discontinuous with the Kingdom of God; the one will not lead into the other; the one is temporal and natural, the other is eschatological and supernatural. It is not by any social technique or political strategy that the kingdoms of this world shall become the Kingdom of the Lord and of his Christ.

At every point the teaching of the Dialectical theologians would seem to reverse the characteristic attitudes of Liberal Protestantism. This opposition appears nowhere more clearly than in their respective doctrines of human nature ('anthropology'). The Liberals believed in the goodness of man, his capacity to know the truth and to perfect human life and society until at last the Kingdom of God is visibly realised on earth. In strong contrast with all such nineteenth century optimism Barth starts from the assumption that fallen man is totally ignorant of God, that all his faculties, including his reason and conscience, are perverted, and that he therefore possesses no point of connection with God at all.[2] Barth's extremism is understandable enough after 'the century of Schleiermacher', but it commits him to an unbiblical doctrine of man. In the Bible the divine image in man is defaced but not obliterated, and even the Gentiles are guiltily aware of that divine moral law which judges their behaviour (e.g. Gen. 5.3; 9.6; Jer. 9.6; 10.25; Amos 2.1; Matt. 5.47; Rom. 2.14f.); but Barth's 'man' is not human nature as thus biblically depicted but is the modern atheistic

[1]   Barth, *From Rousseau to Ritschl*, 325.
[2]   Brunner's controversy with Barth over this issue seems to be a case of the pot calling the kettle black. See Brunner's *Natur und Gnade* (1934) and Barth's reply *Nein!* (1934); also Peter Fraenkel, *Natural Theology* (London, 1946), for a translation of these pamphlets; John Baillie, *Our Knowledge of God* (Oxford, 1939) 17-34; Alan Richardson, *Christian Apologetics*, 127-32.

man, the man who mistakenly imagines himself to be ignorant of God, autonomous, self-reliant, creating his own good
and evil.[1] From this 'atheistic' anthropology all Barth's
characteristic positions proceed: the denial of a general revelation, the Christocentric conception of Law and the dis-
missal of apologetics. His conception of the nature of revelation itself follows no less inevitably. Divine revelation must
create in man the capacity to receive it, since man has no
natural capacity for the knowledge of God. That man knows
God is the result only of the miracle of God's redeeming action in Christ, since between God and man there exists an
absolute gulf. There is only one bridge over this chasm, one
sole mediator of the knowledge of God: Jesus Christ, 'the
objective possibility of revelation'. The mystery of revelation consists in the fact that the eternal Word of God sancti-
fied and assumed human nature in order to become the Word
of reconciliation spoken by God to man. Without this revelation men cannot even know their true predicament; 'revelation itself is needed for knowing that God is hidden and
man blind.'[2] Revelation is a miracle that has happened, 'the
miracle of Christmas'; the *Deus absconditus* has come forth
out of his utter hiddenness and become the *Deus revelatus*;
at the Incarnation he veiled himself in our humanity and at
Easter he unveiled himself in the miracle of the resurrection.

[1] Cf. Gustaf Wingren, *Theology in Conflict* (Edinburgh, 1958),
23-44. Wingren maintains that Barth's false anthropology conditions his whole theology: 'in Barth's theology man is the obvious
centre. The question about man's knowledge is the axis around
which the whole subject matter moves' (34). He remains within
the framework of his nineteenth century opponents (27). His later
attempts to correct his false start are unavailing: 'the removal of
the fundamental mistake would mean the destruction of his
theology' (28).

[2] *Church Dogmatics* I, 2, *The Doctrine of the Word of God* (Edinburgh, 1956), 29. This work is the authorized English translation
of Barth's *Die Kirchliche Dogmatik*, I, 2 (the second half-volume).
The numbers in brackets in the text in the remainder of this
chapter refer to the pages of the English translation.

The Virgin Birth indicates and the Empty Tomb demonstrates that God has disclosed himself to the eyes of faith (181-3). Revelation thus miraculously imparted by God's act in Christ and miraculously attested by the Holy Spirit in the believer's heart thus brings to us the knowledge of something which we would not otherwise have known, even though it is not knowledge in the form of communicated propositions. It is knowledge of God who as the eternal Subject has spoken to us his Word. In the primary meaning of the term, 'the Word of God' is Christ, but in a secondary sense it is right to speak of the Scriptures as the Word of God. We are thus brought to a consideration of Barth's doctrine of Holy Scripture.

For Barth Scripture is a witness to divine revelation (457ff.); this means that it is not itself the revelation (463). God's revelation comes to us through it, and therefore the authority of the Bible cannot be assessed in relation to anything other than itself, for there is no human criterion of the truth: 'Scripture is recognized as the Word of God by the fact that it *is* the Word of God' (537). But this does not mean that the Bible is not also a very human book, having its origin in human historical situations, and therefore subject to all the canons and techniques of literary and historical criticism (436f.). Barth totally rejects the view which today is often called 'Fundamentalism'.[1] 'The prophets and apostles as such, even in their office, even in their function as witnesses, even in the act of writing down their witness, were

---

[1] This title took its origin from a series of tracts issued from America under the general title of 'The Fundamentals', the first of which appeared in 1909. They were written by eminent evangelical leaders (including B. B. Warfield, James Orr, H. C. G. Moule and G. Campbell Morgan) and expounded a number of distinctively conservative-evangelical doctrines such as the substitutionary theory of the Atonement, the imminent return of Christ in Judgment, the reality of eternal punishment, the necessity of personal assurance of salvation and of the experience of conversion, as well as the doctrine of the verbal inspiration and in-

real, historical men as we are, and therefore sinful in their action, and capable and actually guilty of error in their spoken and written word' (529). That sinful and fallible men should speak God's Word is as mysterious and inexplicable as any of the miracles of the Gospels. 'That the lame walk, that the blind see, that the dead are raised, that sinful and erring men as such speak the Word of God: that is the miracle of which we speak when we say that the Bible is the Word of God' (*ibid.*). The revelation of God's Word in the Scriptures is of a piece with the Incarnation of God in human life; the scandal of such an assertion is so great that men will not accept it, and they turn the real mystery and miracle of God's speaking through the words of sinful men into an 'idle miracle of human words which were not really *human* words at all' (530), just as they rob the Incarnation of its real mystery by thinking that Christ could not have been truly God if he had been really man (Docetism: 518). If the apostles were not fallible men, but spoke or wrote automatically words which were given to them, then it is not a miracle of divine condescension that they should speak the Word of God; their performance is not of grace but is puppetry. This is not the way in which God's own revelation declares to us that he deals with men. Barth distinguishes between 'verbal inspiredness', or literalist infallibility, and the true meaning of 'verbal inspiration': this 'means that the fallible and faulty human word is as such used by God and has to be received . . . in spite of its human fallibility' (533).

In Barth's view the true doctrine of scriptural inspiration has been held only fitfully and for brief intervals during the long history of the Church; and these intervals coincided with the ages in which the true (i.e. Pauline) doctrines of

errancy of the Bible. 'Fundamentalism' is thus strictly a body of doctrine akin to the evangelical pietism of the seventeenth century, although the word is often used with particular reference to the inerrancy of Holy Scripture.

justification and grace were clearly understood and affirmed. After the close of the New Testament period, the secular compression of inspiration to an objective inspiredness made it easy to give the Scriptures only a relative authority along with that of 'Tradition' and the teaching office of the Church (519). The Reformers, however, though they retained the language of dictation, restored the mystery; 'for them the literally inspired Bible was not at all a revealed book of oracles, but a witness to revelation' (521); they stressed again the witness of the Spirit (521f.). Protestant Scholasticism (c. 1700 onwards), alas, soon lost this recovered doctrine of inspiration and made the literalistically inspired Bible a part of the natural knowledge of God, accessible to everyone, like a text-book of mathematics (522 f., 525). This was virtually a new doctrine of inspiration, designed to meet a situation in which objective certainty was required by a Church which had no infallible teaching office and was compelled to look for authority elsewhere than in Tradition or the Papacy (525). Since the Enlightenment and the Romantic Movement with its strain of Ebionitism (the human 'Jesus of history'), this kind of Docetism has existed in the Church until the present day as a kind of 'theological bogeyman', which has prevented innumerable believers from understanding the true biblical and Reformation doctrine of the Word of God; it has erected unnecessary barriers between Christian belief and modern knowledge (526). Barth believes that his own doctrine, as thus expounded, restores the biblical and Reformation understanding of the Scriptures as the Word of God.[1]

---

[1] A simple calculation shews that Barth's view allows for a total of only about 200 years in which the true doctrine of grace and inspiration has been understood during the 1900 odd years of Christianity. Barth's long, interesting and instructive excursus on the inspiration of Holy Scripture (514-526) surely leaves something more to be said about the work of the Holy Spirit through Edinburgh, 1960, 446).

We must here bring to an end this brief and inadequate summary of Barth's view of revelation and inspiration, to which he devotes most of the (nearly 900) pages of the second half-volume of his *Dogmatik*. Those who have not read Barth for themselves are often heard to complain of his tedious length; but in fact his writing is clear, witty, colloquial and fresh to a degree which makes his massive erudition readily assimilable; even his repetitions, which usually consist of saying the same thing in a different way, forcefully contribute to the grandeur of the conception and the impression which it makes on the student. We must now ask what is its significance in the development of modern theology. For our present purpose we may affirm that the significance of his work lies chiefly in its demonstration of the truth that the historical and critical theological method developed in the nineteenth century is not bound up with the presuppositions of Liberal Protestantism. In England, as we saw in the last chapter, as a result of the work of scholars like Lightfoot, Westcott and Hort, the new historical methods had not generally been thought to be bound up with the Liberal assumptions; but nothing was known about English theology in the Germanic world of the nineteenth century, and even today most continental Protestants regard the English Church as a half-reformed hybrid from which there is no pure doctrine to be learned.[1] In England, too, the Congregationalist divine, P. T. Forsyth (1848-1921), had already anticipated many of Barth's insights long before 1919 and had broken with the Liberal Protestant point of view which was fashionable in certain Free Church quarters at the beginning of the twentieth century. But on the European continent Barth was the first bold and challenging theologian

---

[1] Cf. Dr K. G. Bretschneider (1776-1848), stung to anger by the diatribes of H. J. Rose: '... the high Episcopal Church, with its Thirty-nine Articles and its tedious Liturgy'. F. Lichtenberger, *op. cit.*, ix.

unhesitatingly to dissociate critical theological methods from
Liberal assumptions and to use them in the construction of
a Protestant dogmatics which is in line with the theological
outlook of the Reformers. He has restored the Bible to its
rightful place of authority in Christian theology, while at the
same time he has not thrown away the great scientific legacy
of the nineteenth century, the critical approach to history.
He has shewn how the Apostles' Creed or the Reformation
Confessions may be accepted in their historic and unreduced
interpretation without making that *sacrificium intellectus,*
without surrendering that intellectual integrity, which the
Christian scholar must keep inviolate if he is to remain both
Christian and a scholar. The new direction given by Barth
to biblical interpretation and theological understanding since
1919 is a matter for heartfelt thanksgiving by many who
would not call themselves 'Barthians' and who indeed would
deny those characteristic 'Barthian' doctrines which flow
inevitably from Barth's mistaken anthropology. No one, as
Barth freely recognizes, can be free from presuppositions; it
is 'quite impossible to free ourselves of our own shadow'
(727). 'There is a notion that complete impartiality is . . .
the normal disposition for true exegesis, because it guarantees a complete absence of prejudice. For a short time,
around 1910, this idea threatened to achieve almost canonical status in Protestant theology. But now we can quite
calmly describe it as merely comical' (469). In the following
chapters we shall go on to consider more fully the implications of this perception; we shall have to ask what is involved in the universal agreement of scholars today with
Barth's recognition that 'the Gospels are testimonies, not
sources' (64). If the presuppositions which the investigator
brings to his 'scientific' study of the Bible determine what he
will find there; if there are no 'neutral' sources out of which
an 'impartial' investigator may reconstruct 'the Jesus of
history' in the fashion of 'objective' biography, are we there-

fore imprisoned within our presuppositions and condemned to utter subjectivism? Criticism has travelled a long way since 1910 and is no longer committed to 'chasing the ghost of an historical Jesus in the vacuum behind the New Testament' (65); but can it be shewn that 'the real historical Christ is none other than the biblical Christ attested by the New Testament, that is, the incarnate Word, the risen and exalted one, God manifested in his redeeming action as the object of his disciples' faith?' (64). This is Barth's affirmation, and we must go on to discuss its truth in the light of the development of biblical studies in the twentieth century.

5

THE EXISTENTIALIST THEOLOGY

As is well known, Karl Barth abandoned his first attempt
to expound his dogmatics and started over again. In 1927
he published *Die christliche Dogmatik im Entwurf* (I: 'Die
Lehre vom Worte Gottes'), but decided that he was on the
wrong track, and in 1932 there appeared the first volume of
Die Kirchliche Dogmatik. Up to 1927 Barth's theology, like
that of other members of the 'Dialectical' school, was cast in
the mould of existentialist philosophy; later he came to see
that this subordination of the Word of God to philosophical
categories was indefensible, and thereafter attempted to
derive his whole theology from the biblical revelation and
to exclude from it all human speculation. Of course, Barth
well understands that freedom from philosophical presuppositions is only a relative affair, since 'everyone has some sort
of philosophy'.[1] But the theologian must know what he is
doing and recognize that his philosophical presuppositions
are only tentative hypotheses, having no independent interest
in themselves. There is no essential reason for preferring one
philosophy to another, and philosophies are to be judged by
the measure in which they help us to understand the Word
of God in Scripture. Barth summarizes his position in an
aphorism worthy of careful meditation: 'if we do not commit
ourselves unreservedly and finally to any specific philosophy,
we will not need totally or finally to fear any philosophy.'[2]

[1] *Church Dogmatics*, I, 2, 728. The whole section (727-36), which
we are here following, is very illuminating and wise.
[2] *Op. cit.*, 735.

In contradistinction to Barth, however, there is in Europe today an influential school of theologians which explicitly accepts the categories of existentialist philosophy as the only satisfactory means of understanding the real nature of Christian truth. Its dominating figure is Rudolf Bultmann (b. 1884), who was professor of New Testament studies at Marburg from 1921 to 1951. He was greatly influenced by the existentialist philosophy of Martin Heidegger (b. 1889), who, before removing to Freiburg, was professor of philosophy at Marburg from 1923 to 1928.[1] With the abstrusities of Heidegger's God-less existentialist metaphysics we need not concern ourselves for our present purpose;[2] but there is one common feature of existentialist thinking about which it is necessary to say something. There are several different kinds of existentialist philosophy, ranging from the atheistic to the Christian, but all of them agree in affirming that man's contact with or knowledge of the real, or of ultimate truth, is through subjectivity or inwardness.

According to the existentialists the widespread positivist assumption, that 'scientific' truth is the only kind of truth, is utterly mistaken. Existentialism repudiates the positivist dogma that any truth which can be known to be true must be capable of verification by means of the scientific method, that is, the method of experimental verification as practised in the natural sciences. Scientific thinking is able to investigate only the external world, the world of things, of *objects* which can be examined coolly and impartially from the outside, as through telescopes or microscopes. Natural science must 'objectivize' and can know nothing of a subjective knowledge, for the latter is verifiable only through personal

1 Heidegger's chief work, *Sein und Zeit* (Part I, 1927; 4th ed. 1935), is being translated into English by J. Macquarrie and Edward Robinson.
2 A lucid and valuable critical exposition of Heidegger's philosophy in relation to Bultmann's theology will be found in J. Macquarrie, *An Existentialist Theology*, London, 1955.

experience, through involvement in the actual business of living, through the individual's decision and commitment. Scientific thinking yields 'subject-object' knowledge; it cannot investigate the personal realm of subject-subject relationships, or, as it has been generally styled since the appearance of Martin Buber's famous little work[1], the 'I-thou relation'. Scientific knowledge yields a vast amount of fascinating information about the empirical universe, as well as a great many useful techniques in the realm of technology, medicine and agriculture, by which we are enabled in some measure to control our environment; but it tells me nothing significant about myself, my predicament as a lonely, frightened individual 'thrown' into the world (if we may adopt Heidegger's language) and there 'abandoned for death'. Scientific knowledge can describe one aspect of the relation between the individual and the universe, but it is not the most important aspect. The vastness of Professor Lovell's universe, like the eternal silence of Pascal's infinite spaces,[2] terrifies us; there could be no hope, no consolation, in the scientific worldview, if this were our only form of knowledge.[3] But according to the existentialists there is another source of knowledge, which we will call 'existential knowledge', that is, knowledge about our *existence,* our inner being, our real situation. This

[1] M. Buber, *I and Thou,* English translation by R. Gregor Smith (Edinburgh, 1937) of *Ich und Du* (Leipzig, 1923). See Maurice S. Friedman, *Martin Buber: the Life of Dialogue* (Chicago and London, 1955), 57-97; a complete bibliography will be found both of Buber's works and of works about him, 283-98.

[2] *Pensées,* iii. 206.

[3] Cf. Tennyson,

> I think we are not wholly brain,
> Magnetic mockeries...
> Not only cunning casts in clay:
> Let science prove we are, and then
> What matters science unto men,
> At least to me?

I am indebted for the quotation to A. O. J. Cockshut, *Anglican Attitudes,* London, 1959, 34.

source is our own inwardness (subjectivity), or our knowledge of ourselves as 'I' in relation to other selves as 'thou'. It is in the actual facing of our predicament—our loneliness, our insignificance in the universe, and the fact that one day we will die—which brings to us true knowledge. Despite the 'shuddering dread', *'Angst'* or vertigo which we feel when we stand on the brink of the chasm of nothingness over which we are poised, as we dare to look down we are brought to a new understanding of our situation, an understanding which effects a real change in our condition. We pass (in Heidegger's terminology) from 'unauthentic existence' to 'authentic existence'—from the condition of enslavement to blind, impersonal forces (popular opinion, the pressures of mass society, the bureaucratic 'state', the conventional ideology of our social group, etc.) to a life of freedom, of personal responsibility for our own thoughts and our own actions, of liberation from the fear of standing alone, of being ourselves, and, above all, from the fear of death. It is by an act of existential decision that we are transformed from 'nonentity' into 'existence'; we become authentic persons. Others would lay more stress upon the importance of the 'I-thou' relationship, the conception of real life as 'meeting,' 'encounter', in this existential transition to authentic selfhood. But existentialists of all types would insist upon the significance of 'subjective' knowledge, as contrasted with merely 'objective' thinking, as the factor which provides such awareness of 'reality' as human beings may possess. Obviously the teaching (and the language) of Kierkegaard is the inspiration of existentialist philosophy, however far such thinkers as Heidegger and Jaspers may have departed from Kierkegaard's intentions.[1]

It is clear that this central affirmation of existentialist

---

[1] See H. Diem, *Dogmatics* (Eng. trans. by Harold Knight, Edinburgh 1959), 22f.; also Diem, *Kierkegaard's Dialectic of Existence* (Eng. trans. by H. Knight, Edinburgh, 1959), 215-7.

thought, apart from any particular philosophies which may
be constructed upon it, is one which is congenial to the
Christian mind, since Christian faith is itself an affirmation
that the deepest human knowledge of the truth rests upon
an inward relation with reality ('God') of an intimately personal kind and that it is not susceptible to the techniques of
verification by the methods of objective (scientific) thinking.
It is verified only in the deeply personal commitment of
trust, obedience and worship. In this sense existentialism
tells us nothing which was not already well known to the men
of the Bible, to St Augustine, St Bernard, Luther, Pascal and
many others. It will hardly surprise us, therefore, that
thoughtful Christians in our day should seek to articulate
their faith by means of the categories of existentialist philosophy. Nor need we have any misgivings about such an
undertaking, especially if the precepts enunciated by Barth
concerning the relation of dogmatics to philosophy are borne
in mind. As we shall see, the categories of existentialist
philosophy may be very helpful in the attempt to clarify and
communicate the meaning of the Word of God in Scripture.
Such a utilizing of existentialist insights and categories is not
in itself a ground of objection to the existentialist theology
of Bultmann and his sympathizers. We would indeed affirm
that there is a knowledge of our 'existence' which is not
reached by the processes and methods of objective-scientific
thinking and we would hold that this is an important truth
which must be taken into account in the formulation of
Christian dogmatics.[1]

[1] A brief clarification of the distinction between 'objective' or
'scientific' thought and 'subjective' or 'existential' thought, together with a warning against the unreflective use of the expression 'merely subjective', will be found in a small publication,
Science and Existence (London, 1957), by the present writer. At
a much more advanced level see M. Polanyi, *Personal Knowledge*
(London, 1958), in which it is argued that 'scientific detachment'
is a false ideal even in the exact sciences; there must be 'personal

The fundamental objection to Bultmann's existentialist theology, which we must now consider, does not concern its philosophical aspect so much as its historical presuppositions. Bultmann's thought remains partly within the nineteenth century Liberal Protestant framework. It is true that he formally rejects the conception of Christianity as a 'positive historical religion'. He is compelled to do this because of his radical scepticism concerning the possibility of our knowledge of the historical Jesus; the long Liberal 'quest of the historical Jesus' has ended in total failure. As one of the leading Form-critics of forty years ago he had reached the conclusion that the Gospels tell us almost nothing about 'the religion of Jesus' but only about the theology of the primitive Christian community (*Gemeindetheologie*).[1] About the historical person of Jesus we can know virtually nothing;[2] it would seem that his mission was to summon men to an existential decision (*Entscheidung*). The historical person of Jesus, his life and teaching, his deeds and words, could not be the theme or content of Christian preaching, whether that of the apostolic *kerygma* ('message'; literally, 'the thing preached'), or of the preacher today, since nothing can certainly be known about them; indeed, Bultmann's Jesus is not a person so much as a 'salvation-event', about which all that it is necessary to understand is that it happened. But, of course, this understanding is not 'objectively' reached as a result of historical investigation, since the latter cannot establish the truth of salvation. It is known only by faith. The Christ who came in the flesh, the *historical* person, has disappeared; but it would not be quite accurate to call this teaching docetic, because Bultmann does hold that it is a fact of history that Jesus died on the cross, whereas of course

participation' in all acts of understanding, but this does not mean that such knowledge is therefore necessarily 'merely subjective'.
[1] Cf. Bultmann's *Die Geschichte der synoptischen Tradition*, 1921; 2nd. ed. enlarged, 1931.
[2] Bultmann, *Jesus*, Berlin, 1926, 12.

the docetists denied this. But the bare fact that a man called Jesus of Nazareth lived and then died on a cross, which can be established by historical investigation, is not itself the salvation-event.

This strange notion that there is practically no connection between the apostolic *kerygma* and the earthly life of Jesus —though Bultmann occasionally denies this assertion[1]— follows inevitably from his historical reconstruction of the development of the theology of the New Testament.[2] This reconstruction is controlled by certain uncriticized assumptions of nineteenth century Liberal thought, for example, that miracles do not happen; in the twentieth century there is a developing recognition that the question whether the New Testament miracles happened is one that can be settled only by historical enquiry, not by the dogmatic assertions of pre-quantum theory physics. But Bultmann moves away from the classical formulations of Liberal Protestantism, which attempted to separate the 'religion of Jesus' from the 'religion about Jesus,' because, although he agrees that the theology of the New Testament ('the religion about Jesus')

[1]   E.g. *Kerygma und Mythos,* ed. H. W. Bartsch, Hamburg, 1948, Vol. I, 149; English translation by R. H. Fuller (abbreviated), *Kerygma and Myth* (London, 1953), 112: 'I do not deny that the resurrection *kerygma* is firmly rooted to the early figure of the crucified Jesus'; cf. also Eng. trans., 44: 'the mediator.... of reconciliation ... is a real figure of history. Similarly the Word of God is not some mysterious oracle, but a sober factual account of a human life, of Jesus of Nazareth.' But in spite of these protests his reiterated thesis is that 'the Jesus of history is not *kerygma*' and that the Gospels do not 'mediate an historical encounter with the historical Jesus.' To understand Jesus as the Saviour, or, in Bultmann's language, 'as the eschatological phenomenon', 'all that is necessary is to proclaim that he has come' (Eng. trans., 117). See the criticisms put forward by P. Althaus, *The So-called Kerygma and the Historical Jesus* (Eng. trans. by David Cairns, Edinburgh, 1959), 43-6.

[2]   See Bultmann's *Theology of the New Testament* (Eng. trans. by Kendrick Grobel, 2 vols., 1952, 1955, New York and London).

is a mythological farrago of Jewish apocalyptic fanaticism and Hellenistic Gnostic speculation, he does not believe with Harnack that 'the religion of Jesus' can be simply stated in such propositions as that God is Father and all men are brethren.[1] Jesus did not have a 'religion' in this sense; he summoned people to an existential decision. Instead of the religion of Jesus, regarded as 'the essence of Christianity', Bultmann substitutes the *kerygma*, the proclamation that the saving eschatological event has happened: 'to understand Jesus ... all that is necessary is to proclaim that he has come.'[2] Thus, whereas Liberal Protestantism sought to extract from the Gospels the permanently valuable religious ideas of Jesus' creative thought, after which the historical element did not matter very much and could be explained away to the satisfaction of the sceptical historian, Bultmann, on the other hand, thinks that the discoverable religious ideas of Jesus, if there be such, are no part of the *kerygma*, which consists not in ideas but in an historical-eschatological event. But, despite this important difference, Harnack and Bultmann agree that the theology of the New Testament in its final development is totally incredible, a 'first century envelope' which may be thrown away when once we have extracted the essential 'religion' or the *kerygma*, as the case may be. We need not here trace the steps by which Bultmann explains the melancholy transformation of the original apostolic *kerygma* into the developed Gnostic Catholicism of the

1 Bultmann's criticism of Harnack may be found in *Kerygma and Myth* (Eng. trans.), 13.
2 This is more radical than Kierkegaard's reply to the historical scepticism of Strauss: 'If the contemporary generation had left nothing behind them but these words: "We have believed that in such and such a year God appeared among us in the humble figure of a servant, that he lived and taught in our community, and finally died," it would be more than enough' (cf. p. 53 above). But Bultmann's historical scepticism is even more radical than that of Strauss.

second century,[1] or how Jesus, the proclaimer of 'the radical demand of God' was transmogrified into the pre-existent Son of God of the later Nicene and Chalcedonian orthodoxy. The defect of the hypothesis by which Bultmann seeks to interpret the New Testament evidence is that it compels him to explain away so much of the evidence itself; Bultmann's hypothesis—that the theology of the New Testament is not the Spirit-guided working out of clues suggested by Jesus but is the work of the primitive Christian community after it had been infiltrated by all kinds of Jewish apocalyptic and Hellenistic Gnostic speculations—does not make such good historical 'sense' of the evidence as the hypothesis that Jesus himself is the original author of the New Testament's bold and compelling re-interpretation of the divine plan of salvation which the Old Testament had already 'preached beforehand'.[2] It is precisely 'within the tradition of the historical-critical and the history-of-religion schools' that Bultmann is vulnerable, a tradition in which, as he himself recognizes, the 'interest' (or presuppositions) of the investigator are not irrelevant to the conclusions which he reaches.[3]

Since, then, in Bultmann's view, the developed theology of the New Testament is presented under the forms of a pre-scientific Gnostic mythology, the only thing to be done with it, if it is to be made acceptable to the modern mind, is to 'demythologize' it, that is, reveal the true existential challenge which is hidden within its first-century envelope. The three-storied universe, with the earth as the scene of a warfare between angels from above and demons from below, has become meaningless to those who think in terms of the

[1] See esp. his *Theology of the New Testament*, I, 164-83, where he speaks of 'Gnostic motifs'.
[2] Cf. Heb. 4.6. The latter 'hypothesis' is maintained and defended in the present writer's *An Introduction to the Theology of the New Testament*, London and New York, 1958; see esp. 12-14, 41-3, 141-4.
[3] Cf. Bultmann, *Theology of the NT*, II, 250f.

modern scientific world-view. The modern man knows that disease is caused by bacilli, not demons, and that miracles do not happen. He cannot today believe in the myth of a divine being who came down from heaven, performed super-natural actions, arose from the grave, and re-ascended into heaven, whence he will return to judge the living and the dead. The language of the Apostles' Creed is the language of mythology; it originates in the mythical fantasies of Jewish apocalyptic and in the redemption myths of Gnosticism. 'Theology must undertake the task of stripping the *kerygma* from its mythical framework, of "demythologizing" it.'[1] The mythical concepts of the New Testament are only first-century ways of expressing the significance of the historical-eschatological truth that the salvation-event has happened and that it is in its inward nature a challenge to an existential decision. The preacher today must express the saving truth of the Christ-event in language which does not offend the intelligence of the modern man, but there will remain the true scandal which offends his pride, namely, the scandal of the cross. It is in order that the modern man may be squarely confronted by the scandal of the cross that Bultmann is anxious to eliminate the adventitious scandals of magic, miracle and myth. Modern man 'ought not to be burdened with the mythological element in Christianity. We must help him to come to grips with the real *skandalon* and make his decision accordingly. The preaching of Christ must not remain myth for him.'[2]

The saving event of the cross is neither a mere happening in past history nor yet a myth; and it is not merely a symbol in time of an eternal truth. It is 'an ever-present reality' en-

[1] See Bultmann's opening essay, 'New Testament and Mythology', in *Kerygma and Myth;* this is the lecture first published in 1941 under the title *Offenbarung und Heilsgeschehen* which precipitated the 'demythologizing' controversy, thus initiating the liveliest debate in Continental theology during the last twenty years.

[2] *Kerygma and Myth* (Eng. trans.), 122.

countered in preaching and in the sacraments and experienced in the daily life of Christians.[1] St Paul has already demonstrated the existential significance of the cross when he speaks of being 'crucified with Christ' (Rom. 6.6), being 'conformed to his death' (Phil. 3.10), or 'bearing about in our body the dying of Jesus' (II Cor. 4.10f.). To know the cross as a present reality in this sense means that we have encountered the preaching of the cross as 'the event of redemption' which challenges all who hear it to appropriate its significance for themselves and to be willing to be crucified with Christ. It is only in its present, living challenge that the significance of the cross can be discerned. It cannot be perceived in the cross as an event of *past* history. 'The meaning of the cross is not disclosed from the life of Jesus as a figure of past history';[2] it is known only in its power in the actual, present life-situation in which we find ourselves here and now, as it awakens in us that self-understanding which effects a real change in our being, the passing from 'unauthentic' to 'authentic' existence. It is this power of the cross as an ever-present, living reality that was symbolized in the New Testament myth of the resurrection of Christ. The resurrection story is a mythological means of representing the significance of the death of Christ. As a mere fact of history the cross could have no saving significance; the resurrection means that the cross is not a mere fact of past history, but is a living, saving, contemporary power: through it we are even now 'made alive' (I Cor. 15.21f.), we walk in 'newness of life' and are united with Christ not only in his death but also in his resurrection (Rom. 6.4f., 11). St Paul has already demythologized the resurrection by treating it as an existential reality of our present being: 'the life of Jesus is manifested in our body' (II Cor. 4.10f.), and we know 'the power of his resurrection' (Phil. 3.10). 'Faith in the resurrection is

[1]   *Op. cit.*, 36f; 110.
[2]   *Op. cit.*, 38.

really the same thing as faith in the saving efficacy of the cross.'[1] Without this resurrection-faith the cross of Christ would be merely 'the tragic end of a great man'; because we know the saving efficacy of the cross of Christ, we know that the cross is the cross of *Christ*. If we ask how we come to believe in the saving efficacy of the cross, there is only one answer: because of the preaching of the cross-and-resurrection, for this is one event, not two. It is a present event, not an event of past history, when it is thus preached. 'Christ meets us in the preaching (*kerygma*) as one crucified and risen. He meets us in the word of preaching and nowhere else. The faith of Easter is just this—faith in the word of preaching.'[2] It is the preaching and the acceptance of the word of preaching that brings us to the true understanding of ourselves by which we come to 'authentic' existence, and then, and then only, we know that it is true. 'The real Easter faith is faith in the word of preaching which brings illumination.'[3] Bultmann goes on to make it quite clear that the resurrection of Jesus, unlike his death, is not in any sense to be regarded as an actual event which really happened, except in the form of an experience of the disciples. 'The resurrection is not itself an event of past history. All that historical criticism can establish is the fact that the first disciples came to believe in the resurrection . . . The historical problem is scarcely relevant to Christian belief in the resurrection.'[4]

It is not necessary for us to enter into detailed criticism of this existentialist interpretation of the New Testament. We will confine our attention to a few of its characteristic features, whether defects or merits, with a view to discovering a more adequate principle of interpretation than that which existentialist philosophy, taken by itself, seems able to provide. In the first place, it should be noted that Bultmann's

[1] *Op. cit.*, 41.
[2] *Ibid.*
[3] *Op. cit.*, 42.   [4] *Ibid.*

kerygma, as he is himself well aware, is not the *kerygma* of the apostolic Church as recorded in the New Testament.[1] The earliest Christian proclamation was that God had raised the crucified Jesus from the dead, and the distinguishing task of an apostle was to witness to his resurrection as an historical event. St Paul, in fact, tells us just what the Gospel tradition was, as he had himself received it, on this very point; it affirmed that Christ had been raised on the third day according to the Scriptures, and that he had appeared to Cephas, then to the twelve, then to above five hundred brethren; then to James and all the apostles, and finally to Paul himself (I Cor. 15.1-8). Bultmann, however, specifically states that 'I cannot accept I Cor. 15.3-8 as *kerygma*' on the grounds that 'it tries to adduce a proof for the *kerygma*', and, of course, the *kerygma* in his view cannot be verified historically but only subjectively or existentially.[2] He sets aside the apostolic witness concerning God's action in history in favour of 'another Gospel', namely, the proclamation of God's action in the existential transformation of the individual believer. Bultmann does this not on historical grounds, since he has to explain away the testimony of the historical witnesses, but on philosophical grounds—on the grounds of his general 'Liberal' world-view, that miracles do not happen, and so on. Thus he remains within the old Liberal Protestant framework and his teaching is a kind of latter-day Ritschlianism: the living Christ is known only in his significance *for me*.[3]

---

[1] The content of the apostolic *kerygma* is most clearly set forth in C. H. Dodd, *The Apostolic Preaching* (new ed., 1944).

[2] *Kerygma and Myth* (Eng. trans.), 112.

[3] Cf. P. Althaus, *The So-called Kerygma and the Historical Jesus*, 83: 'Ritschl's "value judgments" have come back in a new form, on the basis of a different philosophy. The much misunderstood and erroneous expression "value judgments" was intended to mean that religious judgments come into existence only in value-experiences, and that accordingly God is known only when we are aware of the *value* of his saving work for our blessedness. Even the predicate of the divinity of Christ is a value judgment,

Bultmann's view of the significance of the Old Testament is entirely in character with his neo-Ritschlian interpretation of the New. Though he contradicts himself several times, with the result that it is impossible to be certain what he really means, his main thought would seem to be that 'Israel's history is not our history' and that such grace as came to the Israelites in their encounter with God in history is not available for us. The Christian preaching does not, he says, remind us that God brought *our* fathers out of Egypt and disciplined and cherished them in the Promised Land. The history of Israel is not for Christians the history of revelation (*Offenbarungsgeschichte*). Of course, Western civilization has been deeply affected by the course of events in the Old Testament period; it has also been affected by the teaching of the prophets of Israel; but so also our civilization has been affected by what happened to the ancient Greeks and by the teachings of Socrates and the Greek philosophers. Jerusalem is not for us holier than Athens or Rome. Of course, also, we may learn about our own existential human predicament from the study of the Old Testament; we may gain an 'understanding of existence' from our 'critical dialogue' with the Old Testament, and learn about our own historical situation; but what we learn is not different in kind from what we might similarly learn from the 'existential' study of Greek history. It is not at all the same thing as hearing the Word of God, nor is our response to it the response of faith. In the Old Testament there is only the eschatological hope that the existential predicament of sinful man will one day be resolved by the grace of God. It is in the New Testament alone

i.e. it signifies the saving value of Christ for us . . . Ritschl speaks of "value for salvation", Bultmann of "significance for man". The kinship is unmistakable.' Barth likewise speaks of Bultmann's systematic theology and also his exegetical theology as an inheritance from Herrmann, and thus ultimately from Ritschl and Schleiermacher (*Kirchliche Dogmatik*, III, 2, 535; Eng. trans., Edinburgh, 1960, 446).

that this hope is fulfilled; and this fulfilment is perceived solely through faith in God's deed in Christ. All talk of the fulfilment of Old Testament prophecy as a demonstration of the faith of the Gospel is the attempt of unfaith to find proofs for faith; and all forms of allegorizing are foolishness. If the Church uses the Old Testament in its preaching, that is only because it finds in it, though only in a provisional sense, what has now been revealed in Jesus Christ. The Old Testament is not in the full sense the Word of God.[1]

The principal defect of existentialist theology, as regards both the Old Testament and the New, is that it fails to do justice to the historical element with which the *kerygma* of both Testaments is concerned; it therefore substitutes the existentialist conception of 'a new understanding of our own historical situation' for the emphasis upon the divine action in history which is the core of the biblical proclamation in both Testaments. We shall deal with the question of the historical element in the biblical *kerygma* in the following chapter; in the meanwhile we will turn to a consideration of those genuinely scriptural insights to which the existentialist theology has so clearly and freshly re-directed attention. It is precisely through its strong emphasis upon these characteristically biblical truths that the existentialist theology has achieved its considerable influence in twentieth century European thought. It has sought to liberate these biblical insights from the toils of a mythological or pre-scientific world-view by which they were in danger of being obscured. With such an enterprise we have no quarrel; it is as clear to us as it is to Bultmann that many modern people reject Christianity because they mistakenly believe that its acceptance involves the uncritical acceptance of a mediaeval world-view which modern science has rendered obsolete. With

---

[1] The contents of this paragraph are based upon Bultmann's essay on 'The Significance of the Old Testament for the Christian Faith' in *Glauben und Verstehen*, I (1933).

Bultmann's aim of removing the adventitious scandals caused by such misunderstandings we are wholly in sympathy, for it is clear to us also that such false scandals prevent many in our generation from ever being brought up against the one true scandal, the offence of the cross. Bultmann is at heart an evangelical preacher, whose passionate concern is so to preach the cross of Christ in a scientific age that men will hear its challenge and perchance turn again and be forgiven[1]. Furthermore we are at one with Bultmann in his insistence that the biblical revelation does not consist in a number of infallible propositions from which doctrines may be systematized, nor in formulations of permanent religious truths which emerged out of the experiences of a line of remarkable religious geniuses. The 'truth' of the Bible, we would agree, is known to us in its personal or existential significance for our own lives; and if we do not know the personal address and challenge of the Bible, we do not know what the biblical revelation is. It is not enough that I should assent to the proposition that God has created the world; that would make me a theist of some sort, but hardly a believer in the New Testament sense. I must also know that God has created *me*, that I stand before him as his creature, his subject, owing him my absolute loyalty, obedience and trust, yet every day convicted of rebellion, disobedience and unbelief before him. It is not enough for me to give assent to the truth that Christ has died to redeem mankind; the statement is indeed true, but salvation does not consist in assenting to dogmas, however true they are. I must know not merely that Christ died for the world, which I might acknowledge after reading an excellent exposition of Christian doctrine; I must know that Christ has died *for me*, so that *my* sins are washed away in his most precious blood. Atonement doctrine is theology, and I am not saved by

[1] See David Cairns, *A Gospel Without Myth?: Bultmann's Challenge to the Preacher* (London, 1960).

116 THE BIBLE IN THE AGE OF SCIENCE

theology, however correct. The forgiveness of sins by the
cross of Christ is something which I must know not through
'theology' but through the personal encounter of myself as
sinner with Christ as Saviour. Theology, atonement doctrine
and creeds are 'objectivized' knowledge; as such they are
true knowledge; but it is only through my personal or existential knowledge that I understand subjectively and therefore with certitude that Christ is my Saviour, my Lord and
my God. I know this with *certitude,* not with certainty. Certainty is a predicate of objectivized knowledge, certitude of
subjective knowledge. Objectivized knowledge, such as the
dogmas of theology, can never be proved; it cannot be
demonstrated as certain to sceptical objectors. Subjective
knowledge, resulting from the act of faith, commitment and
obedience, alone leads to certitude, that trustful blessedness
which the believer enjoys after he has made his whole-hearted
response to the challenge of the word which he knows has
been addressed to him personally in Christ.

This is the truth which existentialist theology so uncom-
promisingly places before us. Of course, it is not a new perception, but it is one which constantly needs to be exhibited
and emphasized ever and again, since it as constantly becomes obscured under the pressures of formalism in worship
and of the objectivizing tendencies of scholasticism in theology. Such 'existentialist' teaching, though the *word* is no
older than Kierkegaard, is itself as old as the Bible, which
everywhere teaches that God is known through trust, obedience and worship, not through philosophical speculation,
contemplation of 'eternal' truth (*theoria*), or passive acceptance of dogmas upon authority. Nevertheless, because we
acknowledge so much and unreservedly express our gratitude to the existentialist theologians for their powerful re-
statement of the necessity of the subjective factor in our
knowledge of the truth, we need not therefore go on with
them to conclude that a theological proposition can be valid

only in so far as it is an element of the Christian understanding of human existence. Doubtless the doctrines of the
creeds are all related in some way to human existence; but
this does not mean that their meaning is exhausted in their
significance for our existence. To hold such a view seems
rather to turn theology into anthropology, after the manner
of Feuerbach, since it implies that all theological propositions
are in the last resort statements about human existence rather
than about God. To say that if I am to know Christ, I must
know him in his significance for me (not merely as an object
of theological teaching or of historical investigation), does
not mean that his significance ends with me, or with the
saving encounter of other people like me with Christ; rather
it begins with me, for it is only then that I become interested
in the cosmic significance of Christ and understand that he
is the Word by whom the worlds were made.[1]

Nevertheless, even though with Barth we dissent from the
extremism of the existentialist school in turning statements
about God's action into statements about human existence,
we must affirm that in another respect Bultmann's anthropology is more adequate and more biblical than Barth's.
Barth's doctrine of man is, as we noted in the foregoing
chapter, 'atheistic'; he admits no 'point of connection' between God and man; there is nothing in man which is capable
of responding to the address of God. For Barth, man's
hearing of the divine word is wholly the result of the action

---

[1] See Karl Barth's criticisms of Bultmann's 'anthropological'
standpoint in *Die Kirchliche Dogmatik*, III, 2, 534-7 (Eng. trans.,
443-7), and Bultmann's reply in his essay on 'The Problem of
Hermeneutics' (1950) to be found in *Essays, Philosophical and
Theological* (English translation of *Glauben und Verstehen* II),
London, 1955, 259-61. See also P. Althaus, *op. cit.*, 80-9. Feuerbach's attempt to reduce theology to anthropology is well described by Barth in his chapter on Feuerbach in *From Rousseau
to Ritschl*, where he reminds us that 'the doctrine of I and Thou
was put forward as early as 1840 in the strongest possible form'
(359).

of God's grace, which miraculously creates in fallen beings the possibility of receiving the revelation of divine truth. For Bultmann, on the other hand, an awareness of our existential predicament is a pre-requisite for the encounter with the word of truth in the Bible. In this respect the Bible is not different from other literature, or indeed from the record of past history in general. I do not understand the 'significance' of the death of Socrates, unless my own understanding of life has in some measure enabled me, through participation in the quest for philosophical truth in the face of opposition, to relate the death of Socrates to my own existential position in history. I do not understand what it means that Luther nailed up his ninety-five theses against Indulgences on the door of the Schlosskirche at Wittenberg, unless I know within my own life-situation the predicament in which human exist-ence stands before the necessity of making a decision. This is true of the historian's attempt to understand all past history and all the literature of the past; it is especially true of the attempt to understand the Bible and biblical history, which is so deeply concerned with the predicament of human exist-ence. I shall not understand the first three chapters of Genesis if I read them either as an objective record of events which happened thousands of years ago, or as documents illustra-tive of the mentality of pre-scientific man; I shall perceive their significance only when I know that they speak about me, because I know that I am the man created in the image of God, who constantly rebels against him. The Bible 'speaks to our condition' and so makes clear to us the true serious-ness of the predicament of our human existence; other litera-ture and other history does this also, but the Bible especially and uniquely describes us to ourselves and makes possible that new understanding of our existence which leads by the grace of God to the radical transformation of it. But the Bible does this only because we are already aware in the depth of our being of the problematic character of our existence, our possibility of sin and salvation, of life and death, of meaning and futility, of eternity and mortality. It is because we are in the throes of this existential *Angst* that the Bible speaks to us, helps us to understand the seriousness of our predicament and so prepares us for the making of that decision of faith by which we are brought to genuine self-understanding through a right relation with God. Thus, a certain awareness of our true condition must be present in us, if the Bible is to speak to us at all. So long as we are living the 'unauthentic' life, trying to hide from our eyes the horrible truth of our predicament as lonely, frightened beings, at the mercy of vast impersonal forces, standing under the sentence of death, we shall be deaf to the message of the Bible, since it will remind us of those very things which we wish to forget. It is only when we let the Bible speak to illuminate the anxious apprehension which is already present at the core of our being that we shall find in it the way to 'authentic' existence; and thus we recognize the truth of the Bible because deep down in our hearts there is already a dim awareness of our true situation. To this view Karl Barth objects, that since man in his fallenness is incapable of understanding anything at all about his true condition, there can be no question of even a rudimentary self-understanding on man's part before the Word of God in Christ brings to him illumination by the operation of the Holy Spirit.[1] It is precisely at this point that Bultmann's view is more penetrating and more truly biblical than Barth's.[2] It is because of man's

---

[1] K. Barth, *Rudolf Bultmann, Ein Versuch ihn zu verstehen* (Zürich, 1952), 48f.

[2] 'Man may very well be aware who God is, namely, in the inquiry about him. If his existence were not motivated (whether consciously or unawares) by the enquiry about God in the sense of the Augustinian *"Tu nos fecisti ad Te, et cor inquietum est, donec requiescat in Te"*, then neither would he know God as God in any manifestation of him' (Bultmann, *Essays, Philosophical and Theological*, 257). The whole essay on 'The Problem of Hermeneutics', to which reference was made above and from which this

awareness of the seriousness of his predicament, even though this awareness is obscured by his own blindness and sinfulness, that he asks in anguish, What shall I do to be saved? It is because God has made him in such a way that he cannot find his soul's satisfaction in the pursuits and pleasures of his unauthentic existence that he searches for the salvation of God. His search drives him through all the strange and devious pathways of the 'religions' and philosophies of the world, for men were by the wisdom of God so made that they should seek God, if haply they might feel after him and find him (Acts 17.27). But God is not far from each one of us; it was God himself, all unknown to us, who from the beginning put into our minds these desires and set our feet upon the path which leads to him. Barth is right in affirming that without divine grace man cannot come to God; but he is wrong in supposing that the prevenient grace of God is not already at work in the heart of many an 'atheistic' existentialist, or of many an anxious enquirer, long before he has heard or read the words of the Bible. Our quest for salvation, or for authentic existence if we prefer that term, begins with the divine initiative, though it is only when we have responded to God's address to us in Christ that we recognize it for what it is. We know then, but not till then, that our existential struggle was all the time a wrestling with the angel of God, whose name we did not know (Gen. 32.24-30). The God of the Bible is not properly described as *Deus absconditus,* for he is not far from each of us; he is in the place where men struggle to find truth, meaning and value, even though they know it not. He is present at the beginning of man's quest, as well as at the end of it. All existential encounter, like all 'religion', takes place because God is drawing

quotation is taken, is most suggestive and valuable. See also the clear and critical comparison of Bultmann's view with that of Barth in L. Malevez, *The Christian Message and Myth* (Eng. trans.), London, 1958, Appendix II, 168-212.

men towards himself. Religion, though it feels like man's search for God, is in reality God's search for man, even in its pagan and in its most distorted forms. Man, as Pascal noted, could not begin to search for God—or for 'salvation', or 'authentic existence', or 'truth', or 'justice',—unless he had already found him, or rather, been found by him.[1] It is a fact of experience in Christian history that the Bible, the Old Testament as well as the New, is supremely the place where God reveals man and his predicament to man himself; that is why we can hold up the Old Testament, as Bultmann remarks towards the end of his essay on its significance,[2] as a mirror in which we can see our own reflected image. In the Old Testament, we might say, God shews us as in a mirror what we are, and in the New Testament he reveals to us the image of what we shall become, shining in the face of Jesus Christ. These truths, even if they are not always clearly recognized, are at least made room for in the contemporary existentialist theology. The defects of that theology are most apparent when we turn to the question of history and the biblical *kerygma*.

[1] 'Comfort thyself, thou wouldst not seek me if thou hadst not found me; thou wouldst not seek me if thou didst not possess me' (*Pensées,* vii. 553). Cf. also John Baillie, *Our Knowledge of God* (Oxford, 1939), 3-43; *Invitation to Pilgrimage* (Oxford, 1942), 84-6; Alan Richardson, *Christian Apologetics,* 116-132; 220-6.
[2] In *Glauben und Verstehen,* I, *op. cit.*

6

THE 'HEILSGESCHICHTE' THEOLOGY

THE word *Heilsgeschichte* has virtually become a technical term in theological discussion within the English-speaking world, doubtless because there is no precise equivalent in our language. 'Salvation-history' is clumsy and does not convey any very distinct idea. In German the word bears the double sense of both 'saving history' and 'history of salvation', and it is nowadays widely used to refer to those saving acts of God in human history which are recorded in the Scriptures of the Old and New Testaments. The word was first coined in the middle of the eighteenth century[1] and was used by certain theologians of the nineteenth. Amongst the latter Johann Tobias von Beck (1804-78), Professor at Tübingen, resisted the general trend of 'the century of Schleiermacher' by his refusal to ground theology upon religious feeling and by his emphasis upon the primacy of the biblical historical revelation; but his style was heavy and obscure and his influence was limited. Barth speaks of him as one of the 'outsiders' of the nineteenth century.[2] On the other hand, J. J. C. von Hotmann (1810-77), Professor at Erlangen, though he took seriously the scriptural revelation of the divine plan for man's salvation (*Heilsgeschichte*), attempted to understand it in terms of the self-consciousness of Christians; Barth says that he did not break through the

[1] So Shirley C. Guthrie, Jr., and Charles A. M. Hall in the translators' preface to O. Cullmann, *The Christology of the New Testament*, London, 1959, xv.
[2] *God, Grace and Gospel*, 57.

general trend of the century,[1] which regarded Christian faith
as a form of human self-awareness. Throughout the nineteenth century in Germany it was generally assumed by
theologians that the Christian faith could be defended only
by interpreting it as an expression or symbol of the religious
experience of Christians. Faith, defined as awareness of the
Infinite or a judgment of value, was thus cut free from
dependence upon historical events, which might or might
not be knowable to us; it concerned the inner consciousness
of the believer. The existentialist theology of Bultmann and
his sympathizers is the twentieth century version of this
nineteenth century attitude. The theology of religious experience or of existential decision was considered to possess
great apologetic value in an age in which historical scepticism
—from that of the Tübingen School to that of the Form-
critics—had undermined confidence in the possibility of a
genuine knowledge of the historical Jesus; it seemed wiser
to rest the assurance of faith upon the deliverances of the
religious consciousness rather than upon the shifting sands
of historical reconstruction. The quest for the historical Jesus
had led first to the liberal Jesus who enunciated nineteenth
century platitudes about the Fatherhood of God and the
Brotherhood of Man; then to the deluded apocalyptic fanatic
of A. Schweitzer and the 'consistent eschatology' school[2];

[1] *Ibid.*, 67.
[2] This point of view is represented by the 'Bern' school of Martin
Werner and his pupil Fritz Buri in Basel; see F. Buri, *Die Bedeu-
tung der neutestamentlichen Eschatologie in der neueren protes-
tantischen Theologie,* Zürich, 1935. Werner maintains that the
dogmatic Christology of the early Church, which culminated at
Chalcedon, was an attempt to compensate by means of mythological invention for the disappointment of the primitive Christian
community's *parousia* expectations. A 'Christ concept' sym-
bolizing reverence for life, etc., should therefore now be sub-
stituted for the Chalcedonian mythology. See M. Werner, *The
Formation of Christian Dogma* (Eng. trans. by S. G. F. Brandon),
New York and London, 1957.

and finally to the view of the Form-critics that we cannot get behind the theology of the New Testament Church (*Gemeindetheologie*) to any reliable knowledge of the life and teaching of the Jesus of history. None of these appraisals of our knowledge of the historical Jesus is capable of supporting the traditional faith of the Church in Christ as the Incarnate, Crucified, Risen and Ascended Lord; and hence the theologians who held these views were compelled to ground faith in Christ upon religious experience in one form or another rather than upon the Gospel history.

Today there has been in many quarters, especially upon the European continent, a marked change of direction and outlook. As we have noted, Karl Barth became the prophet of the new theological approach, and the year of his debate with Harnack (1923) concerning the basis of the Christian faith stands as a landmark in the development of theological thought in the twentieth century. Christian faith is not founded upon the shifting sands of the attempted reconstructions of the Jesus of history, as Harnack supposed; it rests solely upon the in-breaking of the divine revelation, the Word of God in Jesus Christ, attested by the Holy Spirit in the believer's heart. The Barth of the nineteen-twenties seems actually to rejoice that the quest of the historical Jesus had ended in disillusionment and scepticism, since thereby Christians have been forced back to the recognition that faith has no other basis than the revealed Word of God in the Scriptures, to which the Holy Spirit bears witness.[1] Bultmann at once agreed with Barth in rejecting the view that the Jesus of history, as reconstructed by historical research, could be the basis of Christian faith; but he developed his existentialist theology, as we have noted, along lines which were significantly different from those followed by Barth

[1] Cf. esp. K. Barth, *Gesammelte Vorträge*, III, 1957, *Theologische Fragen und Antworten*, 'Ein Briefwechsel mit Adolf von Harnack', 7-31.

after the latter had made his new beginning in dogmatics with the *Kirchliche Dogmatik*. The combined impact, however, of Barth and Bultmann led to the virtual abandonment by scholars of the Liberal quest of the historical Jesus; theologians were content to say with St Paul, 'We henceforth know no man after the flesh; even though we have known Christ after the flesh, yet now we know him so no more' (II Cor. 5.16). All at once the task of the historical critic of the New Testament had seemed to lose its relevance to theological construction, and a rift seemed to have opened between dogmatic theologians and New Testament exegetes. But such a situation could hardly last long, and today we find, on the one hand, that the disciples of Barth are asking questions concerning the relationship between dogma and historical event,[1] and on the other hand that the disciples of Bultmann are speaking of the possibility of a new quest of the historical Jesus, albeit of a very different character from the 'quest' of the Liberal School.[2]

The twentieth century has witnessed the disintegration of the old positivistic assumptions of Liberal historiography, especially the assumption that it is the task of the historian to construct an 'objective' account of 'what happened' in the past; today it is widely recognized that it is impossible to understand and interpret the past apart from the readiness on the part of the historian to allow the past to speak to him on its own terms, to challenge him to commit himself to it in such a manner that by understanding its inner meaning he understands in a new way his own existence as a being who is involved in history and yet transcends history. This new understanding of the true character of historical method implies a break with the old nineteenth century Liberal con-

[1] See esp. H. Diem, *Dogmatics* (Eng. trans. by Harold Knight), Edinburgh, 1959, *passim*.
[2] See James M. Robinson, *A New Quest of the Historical Jesus*, London, 1959, in which a full and careful account of recent developments is given. See also note 2 on p. 144 below.

ception of the historian's task, inherited from the rationalism of the Enlightenment and still surviving in the English-speaking world amongst theologians for whom theology is still essentially 'historical theology' and who have not understood the significance of the movements associated with the names of Barth and Bultmann[1]. In this connection it is important that the significance of Bultmann's conception of historical investigation as involving an existential encounter with the past should be thoroughly—and justly—appreciated. So often the true evaluation of his thought is obscured by the fact that his own somewhat old-fashioned (as it seems today) account of the theology of the New Testament has involved him in a distorted presentation of the meaning and content of the apostolic *kerygma* itself. Having taken over the old Liberal notion that the theology of the early Church as presented in the New Testament is essentially an obscuring of the 'simple' message of Jesus by alien elements of Jewish apocalyptic and Hellenistic Gnostic mythology, he was forced into a distortion of the original apostolic *kerygma,* which concerned the resurrection of Jesus from the dead, the crucified Lord who is now exalted at the right hand of God and who pours down the gifts of the Holy Spirit upon his body, the Church.

The type of approach which is broadly styled the *Heilsgeschichte* theology understands the apostolic *kerygma* not merely as proclaiming an existentialist encounter with 'the eschatological event' (though this is doubtless involved in it)

---

[1] A clear statement of the old positivist conception of historical method will be found in T. A. Roberts, *History and Christian Apologetic,* London, 1960, 1-48, where a summary is made of the views of M. Bloch, *The Historian's Craft* (Eng. trans. by P. Putnam), New York and London, 1954. Dr Roberts' book might profitably be contrasted with the work of James M. Robinson, cited in the previous footnote; the difference between the nineteenth century understanding of historical method and that of the twentieth century will then become very clear.

but as the testimony of actual witnesses to the acts of God in history for the sake of us men and our salvation. It is not merely that Jesus, who was crucified, lived again in the *kerygma* and in the Easter faith of the Church: the *kerygma* of the Church was from the beginning the uncompromising proclamation that God had raised Jesus from the dead and that he had been seen by the apostolic witnesses. The scandal of the cross, that God's Messiah had been put to death as a malefactor, was attested by another scandal, that God should have intervened in the course of history to bring the crucified Jewish Messiah back from the dead. The philosophers of the Areopagus in every age will mock the apostolic testimony when it proclaims this strange truth (cf. Acts 17.32). Yet the whole Bible and the Christian preaching which is its climax are concerned chiefly and indeed almost solely with the pro-clamation of God's action in history; and the New Testament is centred upon God's culminating action in the resurrection of Jesus Christ from the dead. The *Heilsgeschichte* theology takes the biblical proclamation of God's action in history, not as mythology, not as a pre-scientific way of announcing existential truth, but as ultimate and factual truth. This truth, of course, is not verifiable by the techniques of scientific historical investigation, since the action of God, precisely because it is *God's* action, is not accessible to man's scientific enquiry. God cannot be made an object of scientific investi-gation, as if he were one factor amongst many within the universe; he cannot be detected by telescopes or microscopes, or yet by critical historiography. The *Heilsgeschichte* theo-logy does not claim to be able to demonstrate the historicity of the resurrection of Jesus by means of scientific historical research; it is well aware that belief in God's action in Christ remains *faith* and will never become scientific explanation. Yet it is not mere credulity, since the resurrection of Christ does not lack reputable historical attestation. The Church was founded historically upon the witness of those who claimed to have seen the risen Lord; and apart from the resurrection it is difficult to construct any historical explanation of the origin of the Christian faith, if we have regard to the circumstances of failure and disillusionment in which the earthly mission of Jesus ended upon Golgotha. The historical evidence for the resurrection, regarded simply as historical evidence, is strong; and many events in ancient history, far less well attested, are accepted as historical by historians. The historicity of the resurrection is ruled out, however, by the canon of positivist historiography which asserts that the same laws of nature governed the ancient world as govern the world of today, and that miracles do not and therefore did not happen. But this is not a canon of *historical* investigation as such but is a piece of positivist metaphysics masquerading as science: the historian's task is to assess the historical evidence whether this or that event happened; he may not, *qua* historian, decide whether it could or could not have happened in advance of the historical investigation. The positivist comes to the study of the biblical evidence with his mind already made up; even if the resurrection of Christ offers the possibility of a more satisfactory historical explanation of the available evidence, he will not accept it because he is already committed to a philosophical standpoint which is incompatible with it. The *Heilsgeschichte* theologians, on the other hand, are not thus committed to positivistic dogmas, and are free to enquire whether the apostolic testimony concerning Christ's resurrection does not in fact give a more soundly historical explanation of the origin of the Christian Church than any other hypothesis which has ever been put forward.

We may illustrate the standpoint of the *Heilsgeschichte* theology by looking briefly at the work of three contemporary biblical scholars. Dr C. H. Dodd of Cambridge is largely responsible for having awakened in English-speaking countries the recognition of the importance of the apostolic *kerygma* in the theology of the New Testament.[1] But the content of the *kerygma,* as Dodd explains it, is not at all the demythologized *kerygma* of Bultmann. Dodd seeks to shew that a common proclamation underlies the various writings of the New Testament. This common *kerygma* or basic proclamation affirms that the 'latter days' foretold by the prophets of Israel are now here; the Age of Fulfilment has been ushered in through the ministry, death and resurrection of Jesus, who has been exalted at the right hand of God as the Messianic head of the New Israel; the Holy Spirit in the Church is the sign of Christ's present power and glory and is likewise the earnest of his future return at the consummation of the ages. Probably there are few New Testament scholars today who would disagree with this exposition of the basic proclamation of the apostolic Church as it is attested by the earliest Christian documents. This consensus of scholarly opinion serves to emphasize the complete break with the older Liberal tradition which has now taken place; that tradition assumed that once we have stripped away the theological notions of the apostolic Church we shall be left with the historical objective facts concerning the life and teaching of Jesus, and that we shall thus be able to return to the simple, original religion of Jesus; today it is clearly seen, *per contra,* that the one objectively historical truth which we possess is the apostolic *kerygma* itself: the facts about the historical life and teaching of Jesus cannot be known by stripping away the *kerygma,* since they can only be seen through it. At this point an acute difference of opinion arises between Dodd and the followers of Bultmann. Dodd has strongly argued that the apostolic *kerygma* itself contained

---

[1] Cf. his book, *The Apostolic Preaching* (London, 1936; new ed., 1944). In his *History and the Gospel* (London, 1938) he concisely and cogently sets forth the view that Christianity is in a unique sense an historical religion, depending upon an evaluation of historical events as the medium of God's self-revelation in action (19).

an outline of the life and work of the historical Jesus; a skeleton outline of the history of the Lord's ministry was preserved in the primitive Christian tradition and was used by St Mark in the writing of his Gospel.[1] Not all scholars who may be broadly classed as belonging to the *Heils-geschichte* school would agree with Dodd's claim; the problem which it raises is too vast and intricate for any adequate discussion of it here.

More relevant to our present purpose is Dodd's conception of the resurrection of Jesus as an historical event. What view of history does Dodd oppose to the positivistic conception, which is unable to allow that a supernatural or miraculous event can be seriously reckoned as history at all? He holds that the significance of events as it appears to the persons involved in them is itself a part of history, not something read into the past by historians; and hence 'the best historian of the past is the one who has so familiarized himself with his period that he can feel and judge its significance as from within. Nor does this amount to a subjectivizing of history, since the events of history do not exist as such apart from their significance to those who experienced them, and this significance is inherent in them.'[2] The Bible in both Testaments is essentially the record of events which, as experienced and understood by those who took part in them, were perceived to be the mighty acts of God for our salvation, 'singular, unrepeatable events in which the saving purpose of God entered history at a particular moment and altered its character.'[3] In some respects, perhaps, Dodd's

---

[1]   See his article 'The Framework of the Gospel Narrative' in *The Expository Times,* June, 1932; reprinted in his book of essays, *New Testament Studies* (Manchester, 1953). Criticism of Dodd's position from the viewpoint of Bultmann's school will be found in James M. Robinson, *A New Quest of the Historical Jesus,* 56-8. Cf. also D. E. Nineham in *Studies in the Gospels* (ed. D. E. Nineham, Oxford, 1955), 223-39.

[2]   *History and the Gospel,* 28f.

[3]   *Ibid.,* 37.

statement of the matter is not wholly felicitous. His definition of history as consisting of 'events which are of the nature of occurrence *plus* meaning' obscures his own cogent argument that meaning is part of the occurrence itself; and his speaking of 'an historical and a supra-historical aspect of the Gospel story'[1] seems to involve a semi-docetic belief in a non-historical 'supra-history'. But, if we have understood his thought correctly, these ways of speaking are not necessary to his argument, which is that the understanding of events on the part of those who were involved in them at the time when they occurred is itself a part of history, or is a causal factor in the historical developments which follow. Unless we as historians enter into their understanding of their experience, we shall not understand the nature of the events in which they were involved. If we do not recognize within our own being the truth of their experience, we shall reject their testimony as based either upon illusion or upon deceit; if, on the other hand, we enter into their historical experience, we shall be more ready to regard their account of 'what happened' as basically historical. To believe the apostles' testimony to the resurrection of Christ means to enter into their experience of the 'history' which they lived, to make their history ours. To accept their testimony is neither more nor less subjective than to reject it; each decision involves our whole being, including our powers of reason and our experience of life. The decision cannot be a coldly intellectual one, precisely because a challenge to our whole self is involved in it. This is only another way of saying that the acceptance of the apostolic *kerygma* remains 'faith' and cannot become 'sight', because proof is not possible in the realm of those challenges with which the study of history confronts historians who are compelled to take sides about 'what happened'. All we can do is to try to shew that one historical explanation is better than another, which in this

[1] *Ibid.*, 36.

context means to try to give a reason for the faith that is in us. The opposite of faith, as Westcott used to remind us, is not reason but sight. We may agree with the positivists that God's action in history can never be used as a category of scientific explanation by the historian, just as we would agree with Laplace against Newton that God's intervention in the physical universe can never be used as a category of scientific explanation in mechanics; and our agreement here rests not merely upon our understanding of the nature of scientific explanation but also upon the deep religious conviction that the action of God can never be made the object of direct human scientific investigation. But this conviction does not prevent us from deciding that it is an historical fact that Jesus was known to his apostles to have risen from the dead. This is an historical question to which an historical answer must be given on the basis of historical evidence, and our quarrel with the positivists, if we have one, is their somewhat narrow view of what constitutes evidence. The assertion that God raised Jesus from the dead is not and cannot be offered as a *scientific* explanation, because science, whether natural or historical, cannot investigate the action of God. It remains an assertion of faith, not of faith as opposed to reason, but of faith as opposed to sight. Has Christian theology at any time asserted anything other than this? The *Heilsgeschichte* theology does not seek to claim more than this.

The second biblical scholar to whom we will refer as a distinguished exponent of the *Heilsgeschichte* theology is Professor Oscar Cullmann of Basel and the Sorbonne.[1] All Christian theology, he says, is Christology, and all Christology is *Heilsgeschichte*. This means that he rejects entirely

[1] Several of his works are translated into English. The most important from our present point of view are *The Christology of the New Testament,* London and New York, 1959, trans. by Shirley C. Guthrie and Charles A. M. Hall; and *Christ and Time,* London and New York, 1951, trans. by Floyd V. Filson.

the view of Bultmann that the theology of the New Testament is a mythology and that the New Testament *kerygma*
must be demythologized before its meaning can be understood and accepted by the modern man. 'The question about
Jesus was not answered by early Christianity in terms of a
mythology already at hand, but in terms of a series of real
facts. These facts were events which happened in the first
century of our era, facts which were unnoticed by those who
at that time "made history" and which today can still be interpreted differently, but are not for this reason less historical.
They are the events of the life, work and death of Jesus of
Nazareth, and the experience of his presence and continuing
work beyond death within the fellowship of his disciples.'[1]
Of course, all kinds of Jewish and Hellenistic speculations
and myths influenced the development and expression of the
early Church's Christology, but all such syncretistic elements
were subordinated to 'a Christological structure which received its character not from syncretism, not from Hellenism,
not from mythology, but from the *Heilsgeschichte*. It is
characteristic of this structure that from the very beginning
it centres in a real history.'[2] By means of a careful analysis
of the titles accorded to Jesus in the New Testament (Servant
of God, Messiah, Son of Man, Lord, Saviour, Word, Son of
God), Cullmann shews that the Christology of the early
Church was founded upon the words and deeds, the self-
consciousness and vocation, the passion and death, of Jesus
himself, the historical figure delineated in the Gospels, although, of course, it was only in the light of the Easter experience and of the power of the Spirit in the Church that the

---

[1] *Christology of the New Testament,* 316. On p. 8 (and frequently
throughout his book) Cullmann clearly defines his own position
over against Bultmann's: 'The early Church believed in Christ's
Messiahship only because it believed that Jesus believed himself
to be the Messiah. In this respect Bultmann's faith in Christ is
fundamentally different from that of the early Church.'

[2] *Ibid.,* 322.

New Testament understanding of the person and work of Christ was finally formulated. In the light of the new knowledge from Qumran and elsewhere we must now discard the old rigid distinction between an original Judaistic Christianity and later Hellenistic or Gnostic Christianity; we now know that Hellenistic ideas had already permeated even the esoteric sects within Judaism before the time of Christ. Instead of the old evolution from Judaistic to Gnosticized Christology (Bultmann) we must now recognize the following stages: 'Jesus' life and death, and his own allusions to his self-consciousness; the Easter experience of the disciples; the experience of the presence of the Lord; the reflection, conscious of the leading of the Holy Spirit, upon the connection in the *Heilsgeschichte* between the chronologically separated functions of Christ, which from the point of view of revelation can be extended back to Creation. This development itself is bound up with the central facts of the Christ-event and can itself be considered as belonging to the history of revelation'.[1] In this final development of the biblical theology in the Christology of the New Testament Church, Christ's historical work upon the earth is perceived to have cosmic implications, because he is none other than God himself in his self-revelation. This revelation is now understood to be a revelatory history, which extends backward in time to the creation of the world and forward until the end of the world, and indeed even into the time after the 'final' event: 'the present *Kyrios Christos* reveals himself not only as Lord of the Church but also as Lord of the cosmos.'[2] The New Testament does not intend to supply us with information of a philosophical kind about the being of God as he exists in himself beyond history; its revelation is historical revelation and therefore Christology is essentially *Heilsgeschichte*.

Cullmann's fine and penetrating exposition of the theo-

[1] *Ibid.*, 323.
[2] *Ibid.*, 326.

logy of the New Testament is especially interesting from our point of view, because his work so clearly indicates how in the twentieth century the last lingering vestiges of the nineteenth century positivistic outlook have been transcended. The true biblical emphasis upon revelation as concerned with the mighty acts of God in the history of redemption is once more restored to its proper place; the *locus* of revelation is understood to be history, 'what happened', rather than the evolving religious ideas or the spiritual consciousness of mankind, even though due allowance is made for man's ideas and experiences as themselves an integral part of 'what happened' in the revelatory history. The difficulty about accepting the revelation of God in Christ is not created by modern science or by modern historiography; it is the same *skandalon* as that which confronted the philosophers of the Areopagus or the men of the Enlightenment (like Lessing), and which confronts the cultured modern humanist.[1] It is the *skandalon* which has run and will run all through Christian history. The historical Jesus encountered the scandal when he testified to his own person and work: 'Blessed is he who shall find no occasion of stumbling in me' (Matt. 11.6).

[1] Dr T. A. Roberts (*op. cit.,* 33) quote Lowes Dickinson, *Religion, A Criticism and a Forecast,* 37f.: 'Those acquainted with the nature of historical enquiries, the uncertainty of testimony, the prejudice of witnesses, the doubtfulness of documents ... may easily assure themselves, without entering far into the laborious inquiry, that its results are bound to be in the highest degree tentative and uncertain, that scholars to the end of the chapter will continue to disagree and to dispute and that, in fact, there is not evidence sufficient in quality or quantity, to establish any unquestionable final truth. In an ordinary historical enquiry, this might be a matter of small moment ... But it is a very different matter when men are asked to stake their whole conception of life on the dubious result of inquiries so difficult. And a man who thinks about the issue at all, will, I believe, incline to set aside the whole controversy as irrelevant to whatever is really essential in religion, and seek elsewhere than in history, the basis on which to erect the fabric of his beliefs and conduct.'

As Cullmann says, there is no way of 'proving' the truth of the historical revelation given in Jesus Christ. 'Even today there is no other "method" of Christological perception besides the one given in John 5-8. It was just as difficult for the men of that time as it is for us today to believe in what was a *skandalon* to the Jews and "foolishness" to the educated Greeks. It must be stressed again and again that the difficulty in believing this does not lie in the Bible's outdated "mythological cosmology". The technical progress of our time with its electricity, radio and atom bomb has not made faith in Jesus Christ as the centre of the divine redemptive history one bit more difficult than it was for the ancients. Rather, the *skandalon*, the foolishness, lies in the fact that historically datable events ('under Pontius Pilate') are supposed to represent the very centre of God's revelation and to be connected with all his revelations. That was just as hard for men of that time to accept as for us today.'[1]

The third contemporary biblical scholar who helps us to understand the *Heilsgeschichte* theology is George Ernest Wright, now Professor of Old Testament History and Theology at Harvard University. In his illuminating monograph, *God Who Acts,*[2] he shows that many of our difficulties in interpreting the New Testament are caused by our failure to take the Old Testament seriously; Old Testament scholars and New Testament scholars work in separate compartments and thus fail to make clear how the whole Bible becomes in Christ the source of the Church's proclamation. It is necessary to 'reach back into the Old Testament in order to see what its proclamation of God's saving acts was, and thus to understand what Christ means as the culminating

[1]   *Ibid.,* 327.
[2]   London and Chicago, 1952 (Studies in Biblical Theology series, no. 8); see also his *The Old Testament Against its Environment,* 1950 (in the same series, no. 2).

event in a special redemptive history'.[1] If we had first learnt from the Old Testament the true character of the biblical theology as the 'recital of God's acts in history', we should be much less ready to make such free use of the word 'mythology' in connection with the New Testament. Like Cullmann, Wright utterly rejects the notion that the theology of the New Testament is properly to be described as a mythology. The term 'mythology' has its own proper meaning in the history of religions; in this proper meaning it refers primarily to the personification of the forces and processes of nature under the forms of superhuman, celestial divinities, the gods of thunder or rain, the seasons or fertility, and so on. The development of Israel's faith was one long, unrelenting battle against mythology in this sense, against the baals of Canaanite nature-religion. The outcome of this battle was the emergence of biblical faith, an awareness of 'an utterly different God from the gods of all natural, cultural and philosophic religion. He is no immanent power in nature nor in the natural process of being and becoming. The nature of his being and will is revealed in his historical acts. He thus transcends nature, as he transcends history; and consequently he destroys the whole basis of pagan religion. No force or power *in* the world is more characteristic of him than any other, and it is increasingly understood today that the former identifications in early Israel of a Mountain-God, a Fertility-God and a War-God, from which the "ethical monotheism" of the prophets gradually evolved, are figments of scholarly presupposition and imagination. It is impossible on any empirical grounds to understand how the God of Israel could have evolved out of polytheism. He is unique, *sui generis,* utterly different.'[2]

Thus, Professor Wright is led to deny the applicability of

---

[1] *God Who Acts,* 112f. Cf. p. 24, where he speaks of the results of 'the Christian disuse of the Old Testament'.
[2] *Ibid.,* 21.

the term 'mythology' to the faith of the New Testament, whether the word is employed in one or the other of its two current usages. According to one of these senses, the truth of the New Testament is veiled in a first-century mythology and it must therefore be demythologized; according to the other, Christianity is represented as a true mythology, since it is only by means of the poetic imagery of myth that ultimate truth can be grasped. Whatever truth there may be in either of these viewpoints, they both confuse the issue by speaking of the New Testament faith as mythology; such a manner of speaking is loose and 'fuzzy'.[1] It obscures the essential difference between pagan mythology and biblical faith, which lies precisely in the historical character of the latter. Mythology is completely unhistorical and has no interest in historical episodes and developments. Nature, not history, is the source of illumination, and nature-religion knows nothing of a historical revelation or of the action of God in history. Nature moves in cycles, and the basic concept of mythological religion is that of the annual rotation of the seasons; its cultus represents a dramatic re-enactment of the death of the god in the winter and his rebirth at the spring festival. The older strata of the Old Testament, such as the J narrative of Genesis, have already demythologized the notion that the king is god or that the fertility of the crops and cattle is somehow assured by means of the correct enactment of the coronation ritual.[2] The faith of Israel, as Elijah and the prophets well knew, has nothing at all to do with the mythology of the Canaanite Baal. On the contrary, it is *historical* religion, and the characteristic feature of its great festivals is the commemoration of the saving acts of God in Israel's history, not the solemnization of the rebirth of nature. If God is known as the Lord of nature, this is because he has

[1] *Ibid.,* 126.
[2] See Alan Richardson, *Genesis I-XI* (Torch Commentaries), London, 1953.

already been encountered as the Lord of history; and if the great festivals of Israel's liturgical year are still related to the seasons of nature, they have been altogether transformed by having been made the eschatological memorials of God's salvation in history. If the prophets and psalmists of Israel can still make use of the old Canaanitish myths of creation, in which the dragon of chaos is slain by Baal (e.g. Isa. 51.9f.; Ps. 74.12-14), that is because the imagery has been so thoroughly demythologized that it has now become the vehicle of the worship of the God of history, beside whom there is no other. Biblical theology is essentially a 'theology of recital'—'a confessional recital of historical events as the acts of God, events which lead backward to the beginning of history and forward to its end.'[1]

Both Cullmann and Wright are keenly aware that their understanding of the Bible as an interpretation of God's acts in history involves a restatement of the nature of Christian theology. The Lordship of Christ, says Cullmann, must be explained not in terms derived from Greek philosophy, such as 'substance' and 'natures', but in biblical terms, in terms of 'event'.[2] Wright urges that the traditional conception of theology as propositional dogmatics, or the systematic presentation of abstract propositions or beliefs about God, man and salvation, must be modified to make room for a more dynamic and more biblical view. The Bible does not contain a system of doctrine; it is not significant as a history of men's developing religious ideas; and biblical theology cannot be a systematic cross-section of such ideas treated under the rubrics of a dogmatic theology which the Bible does not contain.[3] Biblical theology is recital of God's mighty acts for our salvation, not a philosophical presentation of the attributes of the divine Being. God is known by what he has done,

[1]   *God Who Acts*, 57.
[2]   *Christology of the New Testament*, 3-6, 181, 235, 306f.
[3]   *God Who Acts*, 33-7.

and the proclamation of what he has done is the basis of Christian theology. It is only by remembering the essential character of the Bible as historical witness that we shall avoid the danger of 'focussing attention by abstraction upon the being of God in and for himself and thus separating ourselves from the Bible with its serious attention to history in which alone God is known.'[1] 'The Church's theology', he adds, 'must always beware of the scholastic tendency to become unhistorical.' Theology in this sense may be defined as 'the discipline by which the Church, carefully and with full knowledge of the risk, translates biblical faith into the non-biblical language of another age'.[2] In our age it is urgent that this enterprise and this risk should be undertaken, since the Church needs today a new dogmatics by which she may understand her own message and her own existence in the light of our new historical understanding of her origin and meaning.

The *Heilsgeschichte* theology thus emphasizes the reality of God's action in the events of world history. 'In biblical faith everything depends upon whether the central events actually occurred . . . To assume that it makes no difference whether they are facts or not is simply to destroy the whole basis of the faith.'[3] Indifference to history is docetism, which is today as it was in the first century the 'arch-heresy'.[4] The *Heilsgeschichte* theologians are not afraid that the most scrupulous historical enquiries will undermine confidence in the historicity of those central biblical events upon which the faith of the Church is grounded.[5] Of course, historical re-

[1] *Ibid.*, 110f. Cf. also Cullmann, *op. cit.*, 325-7.
[2] *God Who Acts*, 108.
[3] Wright, *op. cit.*, 126f. Cf. Cullmann, *op. cit.*, 316.
[4] Cullmann, *op. cit.*, 98. Cf. Wright, *op. cit.*, 127.
[5] Cf. Wright, *op. cit.*, 'We today possess a greater confidence in the basic reliability of biblical history, despite all the problems it has presented, than was possible before the historical criticism and archaeological research of the past century.' Cf. also Cullmann, *op. cit.*, 7.

search cannot prove that God acted in history; but, if it is honestly and fearlessly pursued, it can strengthen our confidence that it is reasonable to believe that he did so act. History points to faith; and faith points to history as the place of God's revelation to men. History does not point away from faith; the biblical history is itself kerygmatic; it bears the witness of those who saw and believed. History cannot do more than this; but it does not do less. And this history is not mythical, but is real flesh-and-blood history, which is proclaimed as having happened; it is part of the actual history of our world. This is the 'scandal' of the biblical witness, as it is the scandal of the Incarnation: that the Eternal should have become historical and that therefore the historical should become the bearer of the eternal Word. The historical Jesus who is the eternal Word is part of the history of our world.[1] The Word became flesh. The factuality of God's action in the events to which the Bible testifies is the central affirmation of the *Heilsgeschichte* school, but it is not a new emphasis which that school has made for the first time in the twentieth century; it is the historic Christian faith. Bishop Westcott may be allowed to speak for earlier generations, when, after citing the affirmations of the Apostles' Creed, he declares that in the Creed itself 'no interpretation of these great facts is added. They belong to life. They are in themselves unchangeable. They stand before us for ever in their sublime majesty, part of the history of the world.'[2]

---

[1] For an excellent criticism of the apparent denial of the significance of this truth on the part of Bultmann and his school, and for an illuminating discussion of the meaning of 'historical' in this context, see P. Althaus, *The So-called Kerygma and the Historical Jesus,* 27-46.

[2] B. F. Westcott, *The Historic Faith,* London and New York, 1883 (fifth ed., 1893, 25f.).

7

THE THEOLOGY OF IMAGES

THOSE who accept the testimony of the apostles that the resurrection of Christ from the dead was a real event in real history would be wise to reject entirely the use of the words 'myth' and 'mythological' in connection with the New Testament and its theology. The story of Jesus belongs to the world of real men and women, the world of Peter and John and Andrew, of Mary of Nazareth and Mary Magdalene, of Judas and Caiaphas, of Herod Antipas and Pontius Pilate, a world of fishing-boats and sabbath meetings in the synagogue, of tax-collectors and Roman soldiers. The Gospel story is utterly different in character from those legendary tales about the gods, the personified forces of nature, which are properly described as mythological, since these do not concern real people or events which can be made the object of historical investigation. The significant feature about the Gospel story is that, unlike the legends of the gods, it is almost universally admitted to be a legitimate object of scientific historical research, 'part of the history of the world'.[1] Historians discuss at length such questions as the connection of Jesus with John the Baptist or with the Qumran sect or whether Pilate really believed him to be a dangerous

---

[1] We say 'almost universally' because the 'Christ-myth' theory of the German rationalist Arthur Drews (1865-1935) is still, we believe, official Marxist doctrine. Drews taught that Christianity was a variant of Gnosticism and that Jesus never lived (cf. his *Die Entstehung des Christentums aus dem Gnosticismus,* 1924, and *Die Bestreitung der Geschichtlichkeit Jesu,* 1926). See H. G. Wood, *Did Christ Really Live?* (London, 1938).

revolutionary; they do not discuss whether in fact Isis found the body of Osiris on the shore of Nedyet or, as Plutarch maintains, in Byblus. The story of Jesus and his resurrection presents us with the challenge of real history; the stories about the gods of mythology do not. What is true of the Gospel story is true also of the Apostles' Creed, in which the facts of Christ's birth, suffering, death, resurrection and ascension are asserted, not as 'true myths', but quite seriously as 'part of the history of the world'. The Creed, as Westcott remarked, does not offer an interpretation of these assertions; it simply recites them as historical events. The implication is clearly that if they are not true assertions, if the events did not happen, then they are meaningless and we are deceived; no amount of demythologizing will give them significance. 'If Christ hath not been raised, your faith is vain' (I Cor. 15.17). The issue is as simple as that.

There are, however, two considerations which have obscured this straightforward issue in recent times. The first is the discovery that the facts about the Jesus of history are accessible to us only through the apostles' faith in him. The Gospel writers were not biographers or historians, and they chose to tell us only such things about the life and teaching of Jesus as seemed to them to illuminate essential aspects of the Church's faith in him. So much at least has been made clear by the work of the Form-critical School. What that School has failed to establish is that the stories about Jesus and the teaching ascribed to him in the Gospels are fictitious illustrations of the early Church's theology (*Gemeindetheologie*), which was not in fact derived from him at all, or hardly at all. This latter hypothesis (as put forward by Bultmann and others) does not account for the New Testament evidence as satisfactorily as does the view that Jesus himself is the real author of the apostolic re-interpretation of the theology of the Old Testament; it was Jesus himself, not the early Church, who first suggested the interpretation of his person and work which is found in the New Testament.[1] If Jesus himself is the real author of the theology of the New Testament, we need not be disconcerted by the discovery that the Gospels present the facts which they record about the Jesus of history through the eyes of apostolic faith. The disparity between the Jesus of history and the Christ of the apostolic testimony will not seem so wide as it appeared to Bultmann and to those who shared his view that the theology of the apostolic Church was an amalgam of Jewish and Gnostic fantasy, bearing almost no relation to the 'simple' existential challenge of the historical Jesus. Once this theory is discarded, the new quest of the historical Jesus may begin without undue forebodings concerning the precarious character of the enterprise. Bultmann's scepticism concerning the possibility of our knowledge of the Jesus of history was, after all, based not upon the 'assured results' of any scientific historical investigation but upon a mistake about the real character of the theology of the New Testament. Of course, the details of the Gospel history can never be known to us with the kind of certainty which we (in our unfaith) would like to have; but a sufficiently accurate picture of Jesus and his work on earth has come down to us through the testimony of those who knew him and loved him best, a picture which has in fact through all the Christian ages proved its power to create in the hearts of believers something of that same knowledge and love which the apostles themselves possessed.[2]

A second consideration, of an entirely different nature from the first, also obscures the issue of the basically his-

---

[1] This is the argument of my *Introduction to the Theology of the New Testament* as a whole; see esp. the Preface.

[2] Even within the school of Bultmann there seems to be arising a new recognition that the figure of the historical Jesus is not, after all, inaccessible. See, e.g. Günther Bornkamm, *Jesus von Nazareth* (Stuttgart, 1956); Eng. trans. by L. and F. McLuskey with J. M. Robinson, *Jesus of Nazareth*, London, 1960.

torical character of the New Testament *kerygma*. This is that the language of religion is the language of the imagination, the language of poetry. It is obvious enough that we cannot speak of ultimate truths, which stand on the frontiers of human understanding, except by means of metaphor, analogy and symbol. Thus, we speak about the creation of the world or about the end of history in figures and images, like the parables at the beginning of Genesis or the pictures of the Book of Revelation. These parables and pictures are not literally true; but they are true analogically or poetically. The poetic imagination is the divinely given instrument by which men are able to apprehend, express and communicate the mystery of the world and of human life. Hence we are able to speak about truths which are not accessible to the methods of investigation which are used in the empirical sciences. It is not, however, only in respect of ultimate concepts, such as the creation and the end of the world, that the true expression of our understanding is achieved by means of poetic images; the language of poetry and symbol must be used also to express our perception of the meaning of historical events. The interpreting historian is an artist as well as a scientific investigator, for history in becoming scientific has never ceased to be an art. Clio, though she has now learned to use scientific methods, is still at heart a poetic Muse.[1] An interpretation of the meaning of historical events is as personal to the historian as a poem is to a poet; it is as contemporaneous with its generation as a ballad is to its period; yet it is as 'public' in its presentation of evidence as is a contribution to a scientific periodical. It is no disparagement to the integrity of history as a scientific discipline to insist that the writing of history involves an exercise of the poetic imagination, because nowadays we recognize that

---

[1] Cf. C. V. Wedgwood, *Truth and Opinion* (London, 1960, 96): 'Truth can neither be apprehended nor communicated without art. History . . . is an art, like all other sciences.'

science and imagination are not two independent and un-
related activities of the human mind but are essentially one
and the same enterprise of the spirit of man.[1] A balanced
interplay of 'artistic' interpretation and of scientific investigation is found in all truly satisfying historical writing.

The writers of the biblical books which record the history
of Israel and its New Testament sequel were not, of course,
scientific historians; they recorded only those events which
seemed to them to possess significance for faith. Furthermore, they recorded them in such a way as to bring out the
significance which they saw in them; they were not interested
in making an 'objective' record of the events for their own
sake apart from their significance for faith. It is the discovery
of this truth which has disconcerted many in recent times
who were brought up in the tradition of strictly 'scientific'
history; the interpretative images which the biblical writers
use to elucidate the significance of the events to which they
refer seem to such modern minds to be purely mythological.
Thus, if the biblical narrator declares that God brought
Israel out of Egypt with a strong hand and an outstretched
arm, he is thought to be introducing mythology into history.[2]
Again we must protest against the introduction of the word
'mythology' into such a context; mythology in its accepted
scientific usage does not mean the interpretation of history,
nor are the poetic interpretative images of the Bible properly
described as mythological. Often, indeed, they had their
distant origins in ancient Semitic mythological conceptions;
but the prophets of Israel have completely demythologized
them and they appear in the Bible as strong, poetic religious
images.[3] When Bultmann says that 'mythological language

[1] See M. B. Hesse, *Science and the Human Imagination*, London,
1954.
[2] For instance, R. G. Collingwood in *The Idea of History* (Oxford,
1946) dismisses the Old Testament in one page as mere 'theocratic
history and myth' (17).
[3] Cf. page 139 above.

is only a medium for conveying the meaning of the past event',[1] he is obscuring the real character of the biblical religious imagery, which is as far removed as possible from mythology in the properly scientific sense of the word. When a New Testament writer declares that Jesus was raised from the dead and exalted (to heaven) by the right hand of God (Acts 2.32f.), the statement cannot properly be described as mythological. Mythology is concerned with legendary tales about personified natural forces, identified with and often bearing the names of the gods of ancient religious belief; but these tales are not taken seriously as historical narratives, capable of being investigated by historical research. The statement of the New Testament writer, on the other hand, is, in part at least, an *historical* statement, one which in principle is capable of verification or disproof by historical method; it is a declaration that Jesus, who was dead, is alive again and has been seen by eye-witnesses. It is an assertion that an event happened, not long ago in some legendary age of pre-history, but in the writer's own day, and that there are witnesses to vouch for it. When faced by their testimony, people accept it or reject it, as with other historical testimony. Mythology does not confront us with a decision of this kind; at most, it asks us to consider the forces of nature or the structure of the world in a vaguely religious kind of way; it suggests to us that its 'story' is in some sense a 'true myth', a poetically helpful way of looking at the world.[2]

Furthermore, the other assertion which is contained in the New Testament writer's statement, namely, that it was by the right hand of *God* that Jesus was raised and exalted, is not properly described as mythological. This, of course, is

---

1 *Kerygma and Myth,* Eng. trans., 37.
2 Attempts to commend Christianity as 'true myth' in this sense fail because whatever it is that they are commending is clearly not the historic Christian faith but 'another gospel'. See, for instance, R. B. Braithwaite, *An Empiricist's View of the Nature of Religious Belief,* Cambridge, 1955.

not an historical statement in the sense that it is capable of being verified or rebutted by historical enquiry; it partakes rather of the nature of an explanation of the historical event which is declared to have occurred. Other explanations might be (and have been) put forward, such as that the disciples who thought they had seen the risen Lord were victims either of an hallucination or of a fraud, or that their experience belongs to the category of 'spiritualistic' phenomena which are the subject of psychical research, and as such carries no more significance than that of other people who have also experienced 'psychic' manifestations at séances and in haunted houses. Different explanations are indeed possible, and they must be rationally weighed one against another in the light of our total understanding of our experience. But in the interests of clear thinking we must rule out the theory that the apostolic explanation is a piece of mythology, akin to the tales about the gods of mythology. The God of the Bible is not the surviving member of the old pantheon of divine beings who once were believed to run the world, to cause the rotation of the seasons, to initiate the new cycles of re-birth, and to operate the movement of the heavens in the days before Kepler discovered the laws of motion. Modern biblical research, as we have seen,[1] does not corroborate the view that Yahweh was ever, in biblical times at least, one of the baals of Semitic mythology; he was a 'jealous' God, and there was none beside him. Transposing this conception into a modern key, we might say that the word 'God', as used in the Bible or by Christians today, is not a common noun but a proper name, as the late Professor Donald Baillie insisted.[2] God is not a class-concept, precisely because he is *God*; by definition he is 'the one beside whom there is no other', and therefore he does not belong to a class of 'gods'. There is no plural of the word

[1] See above, page 137.
[2] D. M. Baillie, *God Was in Christ*, London, 1948, 119.

'God' in its biblical sense. Careful linguistic analysis should soon reveal to us that it is only by an accident of language, no doubt explicable readily enough by history-of-religion methods, that the Hebrew names for God have been translated into other languages by such words as *theos, deus, Dieu, Gott, God,* and so on; all such words are only makeshift translations, and their meaning must be constantly corrected by reference to the original Hebrew, the mothertongue of biblical faith. Ignorance of biblical Hebrew is a serious weakness in the armoury of the Christian teacher and apologist today: 'the Church which lacks the Old Testament again becomes easy prey to paganism.'[1] Linguistic analysis in this context means the scientific study of biblical language with the help of the resources of modern methods in philology, and so on, with a view to discovering what such words as 'God' really mean. It is ignorance of and indifference to such scientific and technical language-study which render valueless most of those articles by contemporary linguistic philosophers on the subject of religious statements which from time to time adorn the pages of the philosophical journals. The only linguistic analysts of Christian 'religious statements' are Old Testament scholars, or at least those who have listened carefully to what the Old Testament scholars say. From the Old Testament we learn that God is not merely the supreme instance of the general class of gods; he does not belong to the same order as Zeus or Apollo, Bel or Marduk, or even the Absolute or the First Cause: he is the God who is concealed from the 'wisdom' of the world which was created by him, in spite of all the intimations of him which are vouchsafed in his world, until he makes himself known to men by revealing his Name in personal self-giving.[2] This, and nothing else, is what the word 'God' means for

[1] G. Ernest Wright, *God Who Acts,* 26.
[2] Cf. Emil Brunner, *The Mediator* (Eng. trans. by Olive Wyon, New York and London, 1934), 270.

biblical faith: the linguistic analysis of a philosophical conception called 'God' is irrelevant to the issue. The God of
the Bible can no more be made the subject of linguistic
analysis (except in the sense of biblical scholarship) than
he can be made the object of investigation by the natural or
historical sciences.

The gods of mythology, that is, the whole class of gods
in the plural, have been disposed of first by philosophy and
then, finally, by the rise of the modern scientific world-view.
The Greek philosophers, who from Xenophanes to Plato and
Epicurus waged constant warfare against religion in the
interests of rationality and morality, succeeded in providing
for thoughtful men a more satisfactory way of looking at the
world than had been offered by the ancient forms of mythological thinking;[1] and ever since their day rationalist philosophers have rendered a like service whenever mythological notions have crept back into religious and theological
thought. The pressure of rationalism is always serviceable to
Christian faith, because it constantly drives the Church's
theologians and apologists back upon their only impregnable
position, that of faith in the name of him who alone can with
propriety be addressed as God. Modern science has com-
pleted the operation, for now at last it is tolerably clear that,
if 'God' is only a generic name for the personified forces of
nature, we have no need of that hypothesis. The 'war' between 'science' and 'religion' has been decisively won by
science; but Christian faith is not 'a religion', one of the
various 'religions' of the world, just as God is not 'a god',
one of the mythological deities who have gone down before
the advancing armies of modern knowledge. We need not
tremble for the ark of God, who still sits upon the cherubim
and still is powerful to save; we stand in mortal peril only if

---

[1]   Cf. H. Frankfurt, *Before Philosophy* (Pelican Books, 1949, 237-62;
first published as *The Intellectual Adventure of Ancient Man*,
Chicago, 1946).

in our presumptuous unbelief we stretch out our hand to protect the ark, as though we could defend God (cf. I Sam. 4.3; II Sam. 6.6f.). It is not we who must go in quest of God and prove that we know him; it is God who calls his people by their name, though they have not known him; he is Yahweh, and beside him there is no god (Isa. 45.4f.). Centuries before the birth of Christ the Deutero-Isaiah was teaching that the rationalist criticism which exposes the gods of mythology as nothing more than man-made idols is not only impotent to discuss the being of Yahweh but, though it knows it not, is actually anticipated and perfected by the knowledge of the one true God. 'To whom will ye liken me, that I should be equal to him? saith the Holy One . . . Hast thou not known? hast thou not heard? the everlasting God, Yahweh, the Creator of the ends of the earth, fainteth not, neither is weary; there is no searching of his understanding' (Isa. 40.25, 28).

The God of the Bible, then, is not mythological and the actions of God in history are not myths. Nevertheless confusion easily arises in modern minds because God and his activity in history can be spoken of only in the language of symbolism. It is very important to distinguish clearly between myth and symbol, for the Bible deals in symbolic language, not in mythical legend, and theologians themselves have unfortunately not always observed the difference. A symbol, such as the Cross itself, for example, grows up out of a complex of ideas and images, and is a dynamic, living form of understanding, of rational interpretation, of expression and communication, and of strong emotional associations and character-building efficacy. The Bible is full of symbols of this kind, and they grow in our minds and take possession of our wills only if we immerse ourselves in the scriptural words and chapters and books, only if we diligently study the Bible with our minds and hearts. This is why there can be no substitute for the careful and prayerful study of the words of the Bible. Even if we do not know the original languages, we can to a remarkable extent learn the symbols of biblical thought from our constant study of the Bible in our own language, for the biblical words impart their own true biblical meaning even when translated into the languages of the nations. Some awareness of the meaning of the original language of the Bible, even though it comes to us through the labour of a faithful translator, is essential, if we are to understand the word-symbols which are the medium of the divine self-communication; and in this connection it is Hebrew rather than Greek which is important, for the Greek of the New Testament is itself only a translating of the biblical-Hebraic word-symbols into the *lingua franca* of the ancient Mediterranean world. The Hebrew tongue is the basis of the scriptural symbol-language, and a theological blunder was committed when it was decided that, if theological students were too hard pressed to learn more than one ancient language, then that language should be Greek: New Testament Greek conveys little more of the meaning of the Hebraic-biblical word-symbols than does the 'New Testament English' of the Authorized (or King James) Version or the 'New Testament German' of Luther's Bible. But in any case the difficulty about the symbolic language of the Bible is not primarily a difficulty about translation; it is the difficulty experienced by men and women brought up in a banausic civilization of understanding symbolic language at all. They tend to assume that such phrases as 'he came down from heaven', 'he ascended into heaven', because they cannot be literally true in the light of modern cosmology, cannot be true in any sense at all. They tend ideologically to assume that the only truths which can be known to be true are those which can be verified by the experimental methods of natural science, and that symbolic (and therefore) theological statements are to be dismissed because they cannot be tested by a logic appropriate to observation, hypothesis, experiment and verification. This widespread contemporary ideology is rationalized in the current philosophy of linguistic analysis, which appears to give academic respectability to the notion that, if the content of theological-symbolic sentences cannot be unpacked into everyday common-sense language or into the language of empirical science, they must be held to be neither verifiable nor falsifiable and therefore meaningless. We cannot speak about anything which cannot be spoken of in everyday observational prose, and (to quote famous last words) 'whereof one cannot speak, thereof one must be silent.'[1] Therefore symbolic theological language is meaningless.

We cannot here embark upon a critique of contemporary positivistic philosophy, but two things may perhaps be said. First, if there are some people (including certain positivistic philosophers) for whom symbolic-theological language has no meaning, this is doubtless a great pity, but it need not disconcert us; it is not really surprising in view of the pressures of modern mass-society with its depersonalized, dehumanized, collectivized rationalism, its absorption in the material world, its veneration of scientific achievements, and its utter religious confusion; there are likewise some people who have no appreciation of art or music or poetry. But there are others who do in fact find profound meaning in the symbolism of biblical images, in theological statements, and so on; and if they are at all given to philosophizing they probably lean away from positivism towards existentialist or personalistic views. Because the biblical images are alive and active in their minds, they find that they *can* speak about matters which are real to them, even though they cannot do so in the language of scientific observation and generalisation.[2] Existential or personal truth cannot be communi-

---

[1] L. Wittgenstein, *Tractatus Logico-Philosophicus*.
[2] For a discussion of biblical and Christian language in terms of the current empirical philosophy see Ian T. Ramsey, *Religious*

cated in such a medium of expression, yet they are not committed to silence, because the language of biblical symbolism
is full of meaning for them; they have learned it from the
writers who fashioned a language to describe their experience
of encounter with God in Israel's history. In fact, they cannot
keep silence: 'I will remember the works of the Lord, and
call to mind thy wonders of old time; I will think of all thy
works, and my talking shall be of thy doings' (Psalm 77.11f.).
But there is always this reservation: we may speak about
God, not as he is in himself, for we have no language in
which we can speak about his hidden being; we can speak
of him only because he has made himself known to us in
his action in history: 'Thy way, O God, is holy: who is so
great a God as our God? But thou art the God that doeth
wonders, and hast declared thy power among the people'
(*ibid.*, 13f.). It is among his people, his own covenant-people,
that the language about God's saving power is spoken and
understood, and it is not surprising that the 'Gentiles', even
though they be expert in linguistic analysis, should fail to
understand the biblical language; it is we, the race amongst
whom God's great deeds have been performed, who love
to tell of them and sing of them. 'We have heard with our
ears, O God, our fathers have told us, what thou hast done
in their time of old'; therefore 'we make our boast of God
all day long, and will praise thy name for ever' (Psalm 44.1,
9). The Bible is the Church's book, not a book of general
religious instruction for progressive thinkers; it is *kerygma*,
recital of what God has done amongst us, not spiritual and
ethical generalisation about philosophical questions. Its
language is the language of a particular people, not the

Language (London, 1957); also his *Freedom and Immortality*
(London, 1960). See also G. F. Woods, *Theological Explanation*
(Welwyn, Herts., 1958); E. L. Mascall, *Words and Images* (Lon-
don, 1957); and John Wilson, *Language and Christian Belief*
(London, 1958).

language of human spirituality in general; it is Hebraic, historical and local, not an unhistorical and ungeographical Esperanto of religious aspiration at large. If one does not trouble to learn the language of the Bible within the community which speaks it, if one will not attempt to understand it in its original, historically-conditioned particularity, it will seem a mere speaking in an unintelligible tongue; there are many kinds of voices in the world, and unless the interpreting Spirit, who is present in the Church, brings home to us the biblical meaning, the voice of the Bible will remain without significance: 'If I know not the meaning of the voice, I shall be to him that speaketh a barbarian, and he that speaketh will be a barbarian unto me' (I Cor. 14.11).[1]

The second thing which should be pointed out in this connection is one which is often overlooked but which is relevant to the discussion, though we shall not pursue it here. Professor Tillich has called attention to it in an essay on 'the Nature of Religious Language',[2] in which he argues that 'symbols are independent of any empirical criticism. You cannot kill a symbol by criticism in terms of natural sciences or in terms of historical research . . . Symbols can die only if the situation in which they have been created has passed. They are not on a level on which empirical criticism can dismiss them . . . Their truth is their adequacy to the religious situation in which they are created, and their inadequacy to another situation is their untruth'. We have just spoken of the historical particularity of the biblical symbolic language and its origin amongst a particular people in locality and time, and we have stressed the truth that apart

---

[1] Cf. further Alan Richardson, *Preface to Bible Study* (London, 1943; 9th imp., 1961), Chap. VIII, 'The new Divine Language'. It will be noted that I have now abandoned the word 'myth' as I used it in that chapter.

[2] In *The Christian Scholar*, XXXVIII, 3 Sept. 1955; reprinted in Paul Tillich, *Theology of Culture*, New York and London, 1959, 65f.

from its historical particularity it cannot properly be understood; we must now emphasize a complementary aspect of it,
namely, its universal character. It is not universal in the
sense of enunciating philosophical generalisations about the
world and human nature at large, but in the sense that it
is relevant to the predicament of every individual person
coming into the world, as a creature who is (however dimly)
aware of himself as in rebellion against the purpose for which
he exists and as helpless to redeem his condition, a creature
whose mortality mocks his longings for eternal fulfilment
and creates in him that anxiety which he vaguely knows to
be the symptom of his estrangement from his own true being
and destiny. In contemporary jargon we might say that the
truth of the biblical symbols—creation, fall, the cross, the
new Adam, and so on—is perceived existentially; that is to
say, in Tillich's language, the biblical symbols possess truth
because they are universally adequate to the religious situation in which they were created. They 'speak to the condition' of men in all lands and in every age of history, including the age of science. They are just as 'true' today as
when they were first created. In this sense they possess universal significance and potency. The rise of modern science
has not brought about a new situation in which they are irrelevant and therefore 'untrue', for the scientific world-view has
merely emphasized the predicament of man, alone in a vast,
impersonal universe which is indifferent to his hopes and
ideals, estranged from himself and from his neighbour.
Scientific knowledge has destroyed his comfortable illusions,
his mythical projections of his own concern across the face
of nature, and the gods in which he trusted no longer exist
to console him. The prophets of Israel did not have to wait
for modern science to tell them that the gods of 'religion' or
mythology were profitless illusions: 'Is there a God beside
me? yea, there is no Rock; I know not any. They that fashion
a graven image are all of them vanity, and their delectable

things shall not profit' (Isa. 44.8f.). Mythological religion was a feeding on ashes (44.20).

The biblical symbols differ from the imaginative pictures of mythology in one all-important respect: they are founded on fact in the sense of having been created in the midst of certain historical situations in which prophetic insight discerned the saving and self-revealing activity of God. These situations may broadly be epitomized in the three great symbol-creating crises of Israel's history: the exodus from Egypt, the redemption from Babylonian captivity, and the creation of a new Israel through the mighty act of God in raising from the dead the Messiah of Israel, who had been delivered to the Gentiles to be crucified. The biblical images, unlike the legends of the mythological gods, were formed upon the matrix of history; they arose, as (despite Bultmann) mythology did not, as a means of expressing the significance of the historical. Without the history there would have been no biblical symbols, for these would not have arisen out of the fancy-free mythopoeic faculty of the human imagination; they are as different from the mythical expression of general religious truth as *kerygma* is from saga, or as the news of a victory is from a general assurance that all will turn out well. We must not be misled by the fact that the scriptural writers sometimes clothe their kerygmatic understanding of what has happened during the history of their people in the traditional religious language of the surrounding nations, by the fact that, for instance, the prophets and psalmists can represent Yahweh's saving and creative act in terms of the ancient mythology of Baal's victory over the Chaos-monster (Tiamat, Rahab, Leviathan, the Dragon, etc.), or that, for instance, St Paul can depict the victory of Christ in terms of the Graeco-Oriental mythology of the captive 'principalities and powers', the world-rulers paraded in the Conqueror's processional triumph (Col. 2.15). It is wholly in accordance with the Gospel of the Incarnation that the saving acts of

God in history should be clothed in the universal forms of the human religious imagination. It should not surprise us that, if the Son of God, when he became man, spoke our language and wore our clothes so naturally that he could be mistaken by men without faith for one of themselves, the imaginative symbols in which faith in him must necessarily clothe itself should likewise be mistaken by men without faith for one of the religious mythologies which have now been discarded in the age of science. If the comparative study of religions has pointed to various images common to both pagan and Christian symbolism, this does not mean that they are merely variant forms of religion in general, but that the divine revelation in history deigns to clothe itself in the common images of the human imagination of all times and places, as once God himself condescended to clothe himself in a robe of human flesh. The incarnation of God in Christ meant, as Dr Austin Farrer has taught us, a rebirth of the images by means of which divine revelation is apprehended, and this rebirth of the images involved the rejection of all that was idolatrous and false in the pagan forms, the veritable recreation of the human imagination itself as a necessary element in the creation of a new humanity in Christ.[1]

Dr Farrer has written with deep insight and great lucidity on the subject of the biblical images, and what he says deserves the closest attention.[2] He holds that 'images are the

---

[1] Cf. A. M. Farrer, *A Rebirth of Images* (London, 1949): 'In agesfor which religion and poetry were a common possession, the basic images lived in the conscious mind; men saw their place and destiny, their worth and guilt, and the process of their existence, in terms of them. Being externalized, the images taken for the reality of the divine became idolatry, and taken for the reality of nature became a false science. The rejection of idolatry meant not the destruction but the liberation of the images. Nowhere are the images in more vigour than in the Old Testament, where they speak of God, but are not he' (13f.).

[2] See esp. his Bampton Lectures for 1948, *The Glass of Vision* (London, 1948), and the first chapter of *A Rebirth of Images*. In

stuff of revelation and that they must be interpreted according to their own laws. The theologian may confuse the images, and the metaphysician may speculate about them; but the Bible-reader will immerse himself in the single image on the page before him, and find life-giving power in it, taken as it stands.'[1] The great New Testament images are the result of the interpretative work of the apostles, who had shared the mind of Jesus during his earthly ministry and who after his resurrection continued to participate in the mind of Christ through the operation of the Holy Spirit. The mind of Jesus was expressed in certain dominant images—the Kingdom of God, the Son of Man, the Israel of God, and so on—which set forth the supernatural mystery which is at the heart of his teaching.[2] 'The great images interpreted the events of Christ's ministry, death and resurrection, and the events interpreted the images; the interplay of the two is revelation. Certainly the events without the images would be no revelation at all, and the images without the events would remain shadows on the clouds. The events by themselves are not revelation, for they do not by themselves reveal the divine work which is accomplished in them: the martyrdom of a virtuous Rabbi and his miraculous return are not of themselves the redemption of the world.'[3] Images are not lifeless

his *A Study in St Mark* (London, 1951) he endeavours to display the unity of St Mark's Gospel as an 'inspired and dramatic presentation of the meaning of Christ and of his saving acts' (7). It is after we have grasped the process of St Mark's inspired thinking that we may legitimately go on to sketch the 'pattern of historical fact' which can be seen through 'the web of inspired interpretation' (9). See also *St Matthew and St Mark* (London, 1954) and the essay which he has contributed to the Eng. trans. of *Kerygma and Myth* (ed. H. W. Bartsch), 212-23.

[1] *The Glass of Vision*, 51.
[2] *Ibid.*, 42.
[3] *Ibid.*, 43. This view is similar to that of Archbishop William Temple, who speaks of revelation as resulting from 'the coincidence of event and appreciation.' 'Its essence is intercourse of mind and event, not the communication of doctrine distilled from

and static, either in the apostles' minds or in ours; they grow into fresh unities and assimilate further image-material. It is in this process that we are to look for the operation of the Holy Spirit: 'this is the way inspiration worked. The stuff of inspiration is living images.'[1] Hence we are not to look in Scripture, as scholasticism does, for theological propositions out of which a correct system of doctrine can be deduced, nor, as has been done in the modern period, for a historical record either of events or of spiritual states in the minds of the apostles; 'we have to listen to the Spirit speaking divine things: and the way to appreciate his speech is to quicken our own minds with the life of the inspired images.'[2] It is the task of theology to analyse and criticize the revealed images: 'theology tests and determines the sense of the images, it does not create it. The images, of themselves, signify and reveal.'[3]

Dr Farrer's exposition of the nature of revelation is important because it carries the discussion a stage beyond the point reached by Archbishop Temple and others, that of 'event' and 'interpretation'. The suggestion that the interpretation of the events is performed by means of the inspired

---

that intercourse' (*Nature, Man and God*, 1934, 316). 'The essential condition of effectual revelation is the coincidence of divinely controlled event and minds divinely illumined to read it aright' (Temple's essay in *Revelation*, ed. J. Baillie and H. Martin, 1937, 107). For criticism of Temple's view see Alan Richardson, *Christian Apologetics*, 145-9. Farrer's view advances beyond Temple in seeing the 'images' as the form of the interpretation of the events, and he is more alive to the danger of creating a dichotomy between event and interpretation.

[1] *The Glass of Vision*, 44.
[2] *Ibid*. Cf. *A Rebirth of Images*, 16f.: 'Christ in his earthly life had made the decisive transformation of the images, and he had given his Spirit to continue the work in the minds of the disciples, to lead them into the knowledge of all the truth ... The images must live again in the mind, with the life of the image of Christ: that is inspiration.'
[3] *The Glass of Vision*, 44.

imagination, and that the birth of the interpretative images in inspired minds is the mode of revelation, is one which is likely to bear fruit in future discussions. Dr Farrer himself has most suggestively analysed the way in which in the New Testament writings the process of image-interpretation has taken place, notably with reference to the Gospel of St Mark and the Apocalypse of St John; it is, of course, possible to approve his method and aim, while dissenting from the particulars of the analysis which he gives, since matters of literary and artistic criticism are notoriously difficult to agree upon;[1] and we cannot enter into the discussion of such questions here. Whatever we may think of Dr Farrer's own analysis and criticism of the New Testament images, we may hold that his suggestion is basically correct: inspiration is not a matter of dictating verbal theological propositions but of creating in inspired minds the images by which the truth about God's saving action is apprehended, expressed and communicated. The recognition of the correctness of this approach could have vital consequences in the life and ministry of the Church, in her teaching-methods, preaching, liturgy and missionary strategy. It also has an important theological corollary. Dr Temple's dictum that 'there is no such thing as revealed truth'[2] may be accepted in the sense in which he intends it, namely, that revelation does not consist in infallible propositional truths: 'what is offered to man's apprehension is not truth concerning God but the living God himself.'[3] But now, if we follow Dr Farrer's suggestion, we must add that there *is* such a thing as revealed

---

[1] See in this connection Helen Gardner, *The Limits of Literary Criticism*, London, 1956, in which important questions concerning Dr Farrer's procedure are raised.

[2] *Nature, Man and God,* 317. Dr Temple explains this statement by adding that 'there are truths of revelation, that is to say, propositions which express the results of correct thinking concerning revelation; but they are not themselves directly revealed.'

[3] *Ibid.*, 322.

truth, providing that we are thinking of truth not as a matter of intellectual propositions but as reality apprehended by the imagination, as God himself mediated to us in revealed images under the inspiration of the Holy Spirit.[1] In this sense we may speak of the Bible as containing revealed truth. Dr John Baillie fears that Farrer's view will involve a notion of the plenary inspiration of images instead of a plenary inspiration of verbal propositions,[2] but this surely is not necessarily involved in the suggestion; Dr Farrer himself agrees that 'to say that the apostolic mind was divinely inspired by the germination there of the image-seeds which Christ had sown, is not to give a plain and uniform account of the inspiration of the text of Scripture, comparable with the old doctrine of inerrant supernatural dictation.'[3] He continues: 'What is vital is that we should have such a doctrine of Scripture as causes us to look for the right things in reading Scripture: above all, that we should look for the life-giving inspired word, and make the proper use of it when we have found it.' The view that the divine revelation of the truth

[1] To say that the apprehension of truth is not a matter of intellectual propositions does not, of course, mean that hard thinking is not involved. Cf. Farrer, *A Rebirth of Images,* 17: 'The work of reinterpretation (of the images) may include much hard and close intellectual effort, there is nothing dreamy or sentimental about it; but it is obvious that the calculative reason alone can do nothing here.'

[2] John Baillie, *The Idea of Revelation in Recent Thought* (Oxford, 1956), 38: 'At least part of Dr Farrer's reason for speaking thus of the images seems to be that he hopes the position he now adopts will turn the edge of the objection to the idea of plenary inspiration. What cannot be affirmed of propositional truths will, he hopes, be conceded to images. This, however, can be only if it is believed that, whereas all propositional apprehension of truth contains a human element and therefore an element of possible error, the images are given directly by God and contain no such element. But what possible ground have we for such a discrimination! The human imagination is just as fallible as the judgement-forming intellect.'

[3] *The Glass of Vision,* 52.

comes to us through the inspiration of the imagination need not and surely should not imply any reversion to the mechanical idea of inspiration, for it is through the work of creative imagination, whether in art or science, in philosophy or religion, that man becomes most truly human and exhibits, if anywhere, that *imago Dei* in which he was created but which through his rebellion against his Creator he has in a serious measure defaced. The study of the creative imagination, of the archetypal images by which man represents to himself his own being, his world, his destiny and the objects of his worship, is still in its infancy, especially in its all-important theological aspect; and we are grateful to Dr Farrer for having pointed us towards a better understanding of the questions involved. The chief question in this field, with which theologians must occupy themselves in the immediate future, is that of the relation of the images to the biblical conception of the Word. Scripture says that the *Logos,* not the *eikon,* became flesh, and that the Word of the Lord, not the image, came to the prophets; Christian theology is a theology of the Word. When we understand the priority of the Word over the images, we shall see the matter in its right perspective. The work of clarification here is likely to occupy us for a long time to come.

8

THE FULFILMENT OF THE SCRIPTURES

THE age of science has been the age in which the human race has grown to intellectual maturity. It has involved the loss of those comforting illusions by which in childhood we are shielded from the harsh realities of the world into which we have been born. For the race, as for the individual, the process of growing up is always painful. As Ecclesiastes, the devastating existentialist thinker of Old Testament times, so clearly saw, 'in much wisdom is much grief, and he that increaseth knowledge increaseth sorrow' (1.18). In the small world of the later Middle Ages, cosily enveloped in its concentric crystal spheres, man was not far away from that bright realm beyond the sky, where hereafter he would receive an everlasting recompense for the sorrows and hardships which he had endured during his brief pilgrimage here below. The rise of modern science, while it vastly alleviated man's earthly condition, robbed him of his comfortable sense of being at home at the centre of the universe; instead of the crystal spheres and the bright heavens above them, it revealed the terrifying infinity of the cosmic waste land. Frightened and alone in a vast, silent void, man has been left to comfort himself as best he may with the legends of science fiction or to distract his attention from his forlorn condition by engaging all his energies in the feverish task of pulling down his barns and building larger barns. The coming of the scientific world-view has brought with it the awareness of the final futility of all man's life and labour and has turned the hopeful, trusting child of the age of faith into the neurotic, maladjusted adult of the modern age, disillusioned, sad and insecure.

> I remember, I remember,
> The fir trees dark and high;
> I used to think their slender tops
> Were close against the sky;
> It was a childish ignorance,
> But now 'tis little joy
> To know I'm further off from heaven
> Than when I was a boy.[1]

The destruction of illusions, however, though painful, is necessary and salutary. The rise of natural science destroyed the Aristotelian cosmology, which the later mediaeval Schoolmen had amalgamated with the contents of the Bible; it did not in any way make the truth of the Bible obsolete. On the contrary, it drove the religious minds of the new scientific movement, such as that of Pascal, forward to a clearer appreciation of the nature of biblical truth. It became increasingly more obvious that what is revealed in the Bible is not a cosmology, or indeed any of the truths about the realm of nature which the natural sciences can explore. But the full implication of this recognition was not perceived until the completion of the scientific revolution through the rise of scientific historical method in the nineteenth century; Sir Isaac Newton did not perceive it, and he devoted long hours of study to the task of reconciling his astronomical observations with the supposed world-chronology of the Bible. In the light of our new historical perspective, however, we see more clearly than he could have done that the Bible does not give us a divinely revealed chronology any more than it gives us a divinely revealed cosmology. We are to look to the sciences for information about the structure or the age of the material universe, because such truth is not

[1] Thomas Hood, 'I remember'.

given to us in the Bible. We are to look to the historical sciences for information about chronology, even the chronology of the Bible, for the Bible is now seen to be only one of the many sources of our knowledge of the Hebrew peoples and the vicissitudes of their existence amongst the nations of the ancient world. Those books which appear from time to time purporting to prove that 'the Bible is true', because some archaeological discoveries have confirmed the biblical narratives, do a great disservice if they suggest that the Bible was intended to supply us with a divinely guaranteed historical record. It is important indeed that the biblical history should be shewn to be a real history of real men and women, and not a fictitious romance about mythical heroes and events; but there is no likelihood of its ever being thought to be unhistorical in the latter sense. The Bible will remain a book of real history, and as such it will continue to be a 'source' of supreme interest and value to the historians of the ancient world. But it is not as a source-text of ancient history that it is valued by Christians; we no longer suppose that the corroboration of its archaeological and historical information by modern research guarantees its supernatural origin as an oracle of divine and infallible truth. Christian people treasure the Bible as the testimony of those who were *there,* when God revealed his presence and his saving power in the actual course of real history. This is the permanent value of the Bible. It is because of this testimony that the Bible speaks hope and consolation to man in the age of science, as in any previous age. The rise of scientific method, both in the natural sciences and in history, has made the true nature of the Bible as testimony to God's revelation in history more clear to us than it had ever been in pre-scientific times.

How do we know that the Bible is true, if its truth is not of the kind which can be corroborated by any kind of scientific research? The Bible gives us no answers to scientific questions; its authors had no access to supernatural sources of information about scientific problems, such as the age of the earth or the origins of the Semites; indeed, it is obvious that they had little interest in scientific problems and had not learnt to formulate them. The Bible gives us not scientific but 'existential' knowledge, that is to say, a true awareness of our existence in relation to God, to our fellows and to our world. It reveals to us our predicament, as creatures made in the image of God yet in rebellion against his loving will, as free to choose the truth yet living in untruth, as possessing eternal longings yet knowing that we shall die. From empirical observation we could learn that we shall die, for this is the common lot of men; from modern scientific cosmology we can learn of the terrifying nonentity and transience of our being in the vast and empty cosmic spaces of the expanding universe; but from the biblical revelation we learn something even more horrifying than this: we learn not merely that we shall die, but that we deserve to die, that the sentence of death under which we stand is just; we learn not merely that we are alone in a vast impersonal universe which is indifferent to our aspirations and our fears, but that our loneliness and nonentity are the result of our self-willed estrangement from our own true being, of which the centre and meaning is God. It is because it brings to us a devastating confrontation with the grim reality of our existence that the Bible is even more destructive of man's comforting illusions and mythologies than is the austere world-view of science. It is thus that the biblical revelation is just as relevant, just as *true,* in the age of science as it has ever been in man's long history. Because it speaks of our existential predicament, not of our scientifically ascertainable status in the world, the biblical revelation can neither come into conflict with modern science nor be corroborated (or disproved) by it.

But the Bible gives us not only a devastating analysis of our human predicament; it gives us also a Gospel, an assur-

ance that God has provided for us a means of overcoming
the estrangement of our being through reconciliation with
himself. But how do we know that this Gospel is not also a
mythology, a comforting illusion of security in the midst of
our desolation? How can we find assurance in that existential
realm which lies beyond the possibility of verification by the
methods of science? The answer lies in the experienced fact
of the saving encounter with God in the events of the history
of Israel and of the Church. This encounter is no myth, but
is a part of the history of the world; the prophets' interpretation of the history through which they lived is just as
much a part of history as are such events as the invasion of
Judea by Nebuchadrezzar and the destruction of Jerusalem
by the Romans. As we read the Bible, as we study it with all
the critical techniques which modern knowledge has made
available to us, we find ourselves standing in the historical
situation in which the men of the Bible stood, and the Word
of the Lord comes to us as it came to Isaiah and the prophets;
the response is called out from us which was elicited from
the disciples of the incarnate Word. I know myself to be the
man of unclean lips, dwelling amongst a people of unclean
lips, fearful of my vocation in my own historical situation,
yet conscious of God's commission and of sin pardoned
(Isa. 6.7f.). I cannot but respond to the challenge of the
historical Jesus and I exclaim, 'Lord, to whom shall we go?
thou hast the words of eternal life; we have believed and
know that thou art the holy one of God' (John 6.68f.). This
is the experience of conversion, the opening of the blind eyes;
it is not the result of human cleverness or insight, for it is
recognized by those who have undergone it as the work of
the Spirit of God. Yet, though it is the result of the present
activity of the Holy Spirit, it is nevertheless rooted in history;
it springs from my encounter through the biblical testimony
with things which have actually happened in history; it is a
sharing in real events, through which the Word of the Lord

came amidst the crises of history, a meeting in the here and now with Israel's hour of destiny, when the judgments of God were in the earth and the eyes of men saw his salvation. This encounter is an encounter with history, not with mythology, with things which once were real to men and women who were just as alive as I am today; their historical experience becomes as real for me today as it was for them in biblical days. Biblical history is something in which Christians participate, not merely something which they look at from the outside; it is a history which they carry inside themselves, because it is the history of their own people, not the history of a foreign nation. It is the history of the people of God, of which they became members at their baptism into the body of Christ.

The special quality of the biblical history, and that which gives it unique significance for Christians, is that it is *our* history. God worked his great acts of salvation amongst *us,* who have been grafted into the Israel of God (cf. I John 1.1-3). Their own history means much more for the members of a nation than it can ever mean for people who do not belong to it, because it is part of their existence; it is that which has determined their being and made them what they are. The resident alien, the stranger within the gates, or the sympathetic visitor, can never feel quite the same strong emotions of patriotism, loyalty and family-consciousness as do the children of the motherland, for the sense of belonging to *this* people, and to no other, is one of the most deep-seated and powerful emotions of men and women in every age. Thus, events in the history of a people's life are celebrated because they are felt to have had special importance in the foundation or preservation of the nation. The stranger, however sympathetic, does not feel that his own personal existence is involved in the historical celebration: an Englishman in the United States of America on July 4th, though with his mind he understands the significance of Independence Day, however kindly he is welcomed by his hosts, feels a certain sense of embarrassment at finding himself involved in a family celebration at which, by the very fact of his own country's history, he is inevitably an outsider. There always seems to be something odd, even faintly risible, about other peoples' national customs and celebrations; and the visitor mildly wonders why such a fuss shoud be made over certain minor episodes in world history which occurred so many centuries ago. In just this way it seems odd to those outside the Church that Christians, when they come together, should read to one another curious old stories about Moses and Pharaoh, Elijah and Ahab, John the Baptist and the Herods, or that they should concentrate their attention almost exclusively upon a particular small portion of world-history and a tiny fraction of the world's religious literature. The history which has constituted the very existence of the Church is not their history, and it seems odd, even faintly risible, to them as outsiders. Thus, Mr J. B. Priestley has written of how the things which seemed familiar enough to him when, as a boy, he regularly attended church services in a Yorkshire chapel, seemed strange and outlandish when, after years of abstention from Christian worship, he visited a Nonconformist church in Birmingham in 1933.[1] It is our membership of the

---

[1] 'Now, returning to it after a long absence, I saw how odd it was that these mild Midland folk, spectacled ironmongers, little dressmakers, clerks, young woman from stationers' shops, should come every Sunday morning through the quiet streets and assemble here to wallow in wild oriental imagery. They stood up in rows, meek-eyed and pink-cheeked, to sing modestly about the Blood of the Lamb . . . They sat with bent heads listening to accounts of ancient and terribly savage tribal warfare, of the lust and pride of hook-nosed and raven-bearded chieftains, of sacrifice and butchery on the glaring deserts of the Near East. They chanted in unison their hope of an immortality to be spent in cities built of blazing jewels, with fountains of milk and cascades of honey, where kings played harps while maidens clashed the cymbals; one could not help wondering what these people would do if they really did find themselves billeted for ever in this world

Church of Jesus Christ which makes the biblical history *our* history and which transmutes a dead record of the past into the living, active reality which determines our very existence and gives it meaning in the present, in the situation of our lives today. The historical commemoration of deliverance which is celebrated in the Jewish Passover or in the Christian Eucharist is no mere memorial of something past and gone, but is a participation in, a communion with, the fact of the divine deliverance in its continuing power, and is an anticipation of that final consummation of this salvation at the last day. History is the determining factor in the Church's present and in the Church's future; this is what it means to say that it bears eschatological significance.

History, moreover, by which the present and the future are constituted, is the sphere of the fulfilment of the divine purpose; the Bible bears witness to the fulfilment of that purpose in the events which it records. The argument from the fulfilment of the Scriptures has always been one of the strongest weapons in the armoury of the Christian apologist. Not that 'arguments', of course, can ever of themselves convince unbelievers, but they can powerfully support the conviction of Christians that they have not believed in vain. The argument from the fulfilment of the Scriptures can be restated today in the light of our new historical knowledge with greater cogency than it has ever previously possessed. But it

of the Eastern religious poets. What, in short, had these sober Northern islanders to do with all this Oriental stuff? What did it, what could it really mean to them? Could anything be less aptly shaped and coloured to match their own lives? If this was the time when their thoughts turned to the creator of this universe, when they were asked to consider the deep truths of life, to face their consciences and search their hearts, why should they be dragged into this far-away fantastic world of goats and vines and deserts and smoking sacrifices and tribal kings? ... Must God, I asked myself, remain for ever in Asia? Are these people always to assume that he is still brooding over Babylon? What if he is now brooding over Birmingham?' (*English Journey*, 1934, 109f.).

should now be stated in the form of fulfilment in history, not merely as a fulfilment of ideas or images or literary forms.[1] What is primary is the saving events themselves; the images and ideas which arose out of the events are, of course, very important, but they are nevertheless only secondary. It was the experience of redemption, the fact of the actual, historic deliverance of Israel from Egyptian oppression at the Exodus, which gave birth to the great biblical images of God as Israel's *go'el* or Redeemer, and which led Israel, despite her faithlessness, to trust in his deliverance and to celebrate the Passover in expectation of the Messianic redemption that was to come. It was the historical events which gave rise to Israel's faith, not faith which gave rise to myths and legends about the crossing of the Red Sea and the wonders in the desert. The historical reality can account for Israel's faith and for its persistence for a thousand years in spite of and in opposition to the seductions of Canaanite religion and in spite of the temptation to unbelief when the gods of the Philistines or of Assyria or Babylon had apparently triumphed over Yahweh. Nothing but the historical reality of the Exodus as an overpowering experience of divine deliverance can account for the *sui generis* character of Israel's faith; apart from Israel's experience in history the faith of Israel is inexplicable. It was the fulfilment of this faith, which had arisen out of Israel's history, that brought into being the Christian Church; the earliest Christian proclamation affirmed that the promise of Israel's history was fulfilled in the life, death and exaltation of Jesus Christ. This faith, that

[1]   H. P. Liddon, it will be recalled, argued in 1866 for a kind of *literary* fulfilment of the Scriptures, which revealed behind them 'the continuous action of a Single Mind' (see Chapter III above, pp. 71f.). He was arguing in terms of a concept of *inspiration*. This kind of argument can still be validly used, but today in the light of our conception of revelation in history it is clearly of secondary importance; the primary truth is that of fulfilment in events, not in literature.

Jesus Christ was the fulfilment of the Scriptures, was itself, like the faith of Israel of old, based upon historical events, and without those events it is equally inexplicable. Apart from the resurrection of Jesus it is inconceivable that a group of Jews would ever have come to believe that the Law and the Prophets of Israel had been fulfilled in a working-class Messianic pretender who had been executed by the Roman governor. The event of the resurrection can account for the rise of the Christian faith; but how can we ever explain the origin of the belief that Israel's historic destiny had been fulfilled by the hypothesis of a Messiah who suffered under Pontius Pilate, was crucified, dead and buried, and whose corpse lay mouldering in a grave owned by one of the members of the Sanhedrin? The events precede the faith and account for its rise; it cannot be the faith which gave rise to myths and legends about fictitious events; a cause can explain an effect, but an effect will not explain a cause.

The Bible itself provides evidence that faith was created by events, because in both Testaments the expressions of faith, or credal confessions, take the form of a recitation of the saving acts of God, and the biblical theology is essentially a *kerygma*; in Professor Wright's phrase it is 'a theology of recital'. The oldest confessions of Israel's faith which we find in the Old Testament refer explicitly to God's great, saving act in delivering Israel from bondage in Egypt. Professor Gerhard von Rad has noted that in the Hexateuch there is a whole collection of shorter or longer passages which take the form of a confessional recitation of God's historical redemption of his people.[1] For instance, when the Israelite comes to the Temple to make his offering of the firstfruits, while the priest sets down his basket before the altar, he is instructed to say: 'A Syrian ready to perish was

[1]   G. von Rad, *Das erste Buch Mose* (Genesis 1-12.9), Das Alte Testament Deutsch, I, Göttingen, 1949, 8f. An English translation (in Old Testament Library) is in preparation.

my father, and he went down to Egypt and sojourned there . . . and the Egyptians evil entreated us . . . and laid upon us hard bondage; and we cried unto Yahweh, the God of our fathers, and Yahweh heard our voice . . . and brought us forth out of Egypt with a mighty hand and with an outstretched arm . . . and hath given us this land, a land flowing with milk and honey' (Deut. 26.5-9; cf. also 6.20-24; Joshua 24.2-13). In this remarkable confession we see how even the harvest-thanksgiving, which might so easily have been a mere expression of nature-religion, is turned into a commemoration of God's saving act in history: God is thanked not simply as the beneficent provider of the fruits of the earth in their season but as the Deliverer at the Red Sea; it is the God of history, not the fertility god, who is in the mind of the offerer. As von Rad says, we have here the recitation of a short version of the *Heilsgeschichte,* a kind of *Credo,* a personal prayer of thanksgiving for Israel's deliverance and preservation. 'The speaker recapitulates the great fact of salvation, by which the community (*Gemeinde*) has been constituted. He abandons every concern of his own and at this moment identifies himself completely with the *Gemeinde*; that is to say, he utters a Confession (*Bekenntnis*)'.[1] The experience of deliverance which his forefathers have undergone has entered into the very being of the individual Israelite, given to him the strong sense of belonging to a people with an historical destiny and mission, and thus has delivered him from frustration, loneliness and futility. History has determined his very existence, and his fathers' experience of encounter with the Lord of history has become his own personal means of encounter with Israel's God. It is not dead history but living history; it is his own history. It belongs to him and he belongs to it. This is the sense in which biblical faith may be described as 'historical', and it is this historical character which distinguishes the Bible from all

[1]   *Ibid.,* 8.

(non-historical) 'religion'. The God of the harvest, to whom it is meet to present the firstfruits of the harvest, is the God of history. How often in our modern churches do our 'harvest festivals' approximate to pagan nature-religion because we have neglected the Old Testament! The connection between the harvest and the *kerygma* is not very obvious in some of our present-day services, and yet we flatter ourselves that we have advanced beyond the 'primitive' ideas of the Hexateuch.

Throughout the Old Testament the worship of Israel resounds with the praises of God for his mighty acts in Israel's history, and the Psalmists constantly recite his saving deeds (e.g. Pss. 44.1-8; 78; 105; 106; 114; 126; 135; 136). The Passover was the annual historical-eschatological re-enactment of the Deliverance from Egypt, regarded as the type of the coming great salvation. Pentecost celebrated the giving of the Law on Sinai, and the Feast of Tabernacles commemorated the days when Israel dwelt in tents in the Wilderness. The New Testament takes up the story of God's saving activity, and proclaims the fulfilment of what had been foreshadowed and promised in the acts of God in Israel's history. The great salvation, of which the deliverance from Egypt was the historical 'type' or foreshadowing, was now achieved in the coming of Israel's Messiah, who through his death and resurrection had accomplished a new 'exodus' in Jerusalem (Luke 9.31); and the final deliverance thus effected was celebrated in the Church's Eucharist, the Christian Passover, which, like the Jewish Passover-commemoration, was at once the recalling and making present of historical events (I Cor. 11.23-26) and an anticipation of the consummation of history in the Kingdom of God: 'as often as ye eat this bread and drink the cup, ye proclaim the Lord's death till he come' (I Cor. 11.26). The earliest Christian worship was centred upon the sacrifice and exaltation of Christ as the events which were constitutive of the very existence of the Church (e.g. Acts 4.24-30; Phil. 2.5-11;

Rev. 5.12-14; 15.3f.). The earliest Christian creeds were concerned almost exclusively with the acts of God wrought by the historical Christ.[1] The Apostles' Creed was gradually developed out of the older forms of baptismal creed as a summary of the scriptural teaching concerning God's culminating action in history for the salvation of mankind. The Nicene Creed in its developed conciliar form has not merely been treated by the Church down the centuries as a compendium of systematic theology but has rather been sung as a hymn of praise in Christian worship, a Christian psalm of thanksgiving for the revelation of God, the Father Almighty, Maker of all things visible and invisible, who in his only-begotten Son, Jesus Christ, of one substance with himself, was made man for the sake of us men and for our salvation, born, crucified, risen and ascended. The credal confessions of the New Israel, like those of the old Israel, are recitations of the *kerygma,* hymns of thanksgiving for the saving work of God in history. They are, as Christians believe, inspired by that same Holy Spirit of God who formerly spoke by the prophets of Israel and revealed to them the true meaning of the decisive historical events which had taken place in their own days.

We may, if we wish, speak of this kind of fulfilment of Old Testament prophecy in the New Testament as typological. But we must stress the fact that Old Testament prophecy is not primarily verbal, a matter of oracles concerning the future which were later seen to have been correct. It is the Old Testament history itself which is prophetic; it came increasingly to be understood by the prophets of Israel as carrying within itself the promise of that final salvation

[1] Cf. O. Cullmann, *The Earliest Christian Confessions* (Eng. trans. by J. K. S. Reid, London, 1949), 57: 'We can conclude that the divine Sonship of Jesus Christ and his elevation to the dignity of *Kyrios,* as a consequence of his death and resurrection, are the two essential elements in the majority of the confessions of the first century.'

which it foreshadowed. Because God had given the sign in history that he was the Redeemer of his people, and because, being God, he must remain true to his covenant and promise, therefore he would not suffer them to be destroyed but would come amongst them once more and visit them with his salvation. It was not that the prophets were inspired to utter oracles about future events, like pagan seers peering into a crystal, but that they were inspired to understand God's action in the events of their people's history and in the crises of their own days, so that they could assert with confidence the pattern and plan of God's judgment and salvation in the time to come. Because God had revealed himself in action, they discerned, however dimly, the purpose of his great design. Thus there arose in Israel that unique phenomenon in the history of religion, a line of prophets who could interpret to those who would hearken what God was doing in their own days and what he would do hereafter: 'since the day that your fathers came forth out of the land of Egypt unto this day, I have sent unto you all my servants the prophets, daily rising up early and sending them' (Jer. 7.25). Thus, history itself becomes prophetic; what God has done is the clue to what he will do. It is because of his dealings with his people in history, not as the result of speculation upon the being and attributes of God, that the Bible can declare him to be 'a God full of compassion and gracious, slow to anger and plenteous in mercy and truth; keeping mercy (ḥesed) for thousands, forgiving iniquity, transgression and sin' (Ex. 34.6f.).[1] It is because God's promise, implicit in his dealings with his people under the old Covenant, is fulfilled in the coming of Jesus and his Church that we can speak of a biblical typology, a fulfilment of those historical type-situations (such as the Deliverance from Egypt), about which the Old Testament informs us, in the historical events which the New Testament declares.

[1]   Cf. G. E. Wright, *God Who Acts*, 85.

Thus typology, properly understood, is, as Professor Lampe has written, 'grounded in a particular view of history which the New Testament writers undoubtedly held themselves and which Christians for whom the Bible is authoritative can scarcely repudiate . . . It is a secret in the counsel of God which is being made known in Christ, an element in the hidden purpose of God which has been made manifest in being fulfilled . . . There is a real correspondence between the type in the past and the fulfilment in the future. Typology of this kind is an expression of the particular view of history held by the scriptural writers as a whole, and in this expression the type is a genuine foreshadowing.'[1] Such typology has nothing in common with old allegorical method of scriptural interpretation, which is fanciful, uncritical and unhistorical.[2] All that is meant by typology is that the New Testament writers see in the events of the life, death and resurrection of Jesus the fulfilment of those historical situations in Israel's past in which already the saving purpose of God had been disclosed. They interpret the past in the light of the present, for now they see clearly the true significance of what had formerly been discerned only dimly. This

[1] *Essays on Typology* by G. W. H. Lampe and K. J. Woollcombe (Studies in Biblical Theology, 22), London, 1957, 29f.

[2] Cf. G. W. H. Lampe, *op. cit.* 31: 'The conception of Scripture as a single vast volume of oracles and riddles, a huge book of secret puzzles to which the reader has to find clues, is the foundation of allegorical exegesis. Allegory differs radically from the kind of typology which rests upon the perception of actual historical fulfilment. The reason for this great difference is simply that allegory takes no account of history. The exegete has to penetrate through the shell of history to the inner kernel of eternal spiritual or moral truth.' Cf. also the distinction drawn by Dr R. P. C. Hanson (*Allegory and Event,* London, 1959, 7): 'Typology is the interpreting of an event belonging to the present or the recent past as the fulfilment of a similar situation recorded or prophesied in Scripture. Allegory is the interpretation of an object or person . . . as in reality meaning some object or person of a later time, with no attempt to trace a relationship of "similar situation" between them.'

THE FULFILMENT OF THE SCRIPTURES

was not a new method of interpreting history which the primitive Church had discovered; it had already been used by the prophets and theologians of Israel, who had interpreted the meaning of God's action in the past in the light of their understanding of later events. Thus, the Deutero-Isaiah understood the Return from Exile as a typological fulfilment of the Exodus from Egypt (Isa. 43.14-21), which in its turn was itself a typological fulfilment of God's original act of redemption from Chaos in the creation (Isa. 51.9-11; cf. Ps. 74.12-14; Wisd. 19.6-22). Or again, as Professor Knight has pointed out, the P writer of the Old Testament understood the significance of the Tabernacle in the Wilderness wanderings in the light of his fully developed conception of the Temple in Jerusalem; his theology of the Tabernacle was 'created by one who already knew the end of the process of theological growth and development and who could thus see the significance of the beginning from the end.'[1] Such typology, says Professor Knight, is a legitimate method of interpretation; it is only from the vantage point of the end of an historical development that we can properly understand the significance of the events which occurred at the beginning and during the course of it. It is in this way that the New Testament understands the significance of the Old Testament history. It can now be properly seen in the light of its fulfilment in Christ.[2]

[1] G. A. F. Knight, *A Christian Theology of the Old Testament*, London, 1959, 216.
[2] It is because Professor Knight shews this truth so clearly that his book, mentioned in the previous footnote, is the best students' and preachers' introduction to the theology of the Old Testament which has so far been published. It is much to be hoped that teachers, when introducing students to the modern study of the Old Testament, will start their courses from the very beginning with this kind of emphasis upon its theological and Christian significance. Students will then see *why* it is important that they should master the critical problems involved. In the past the Old Testament has all too frequently been taught in such a way that

It is important to understand that the New Testament writers read the Old Testament story in the light of the revelation of God in the Jesus of history; they do not construct a fanciful Christ of the imagination out of an amalgam of Old Testament types and figures. It is the historical Jesus who interprets the Scriptures, the Jesus who was born of Mary, baptized by John the Baptist, followed by Peter and Andrew, betrayed by Judas, crucified by Pontius Pilate, and raised from the dead by God himself. In this story of the historical Jesus the history of Israel is fulfilled. Jesus is himself the true Israel, the Son of God and Servant of the Lord, whose mission and task has been triumphantly accomplished, where the old Israel, God's 'Son' and 'Servant', had ignominiously failed. The Old Israel had indeed foreshadowed but had not realised the salvation in history which God had purposed for mankind. In the actual history of Israel can be seen the pattern of that redemption which was afterwards fulfilled in the life and work of the Jesus of history, and there is no need to resort to far-fetched allegorical interpretation to prove that a pattern is there; the critical study of the Old Testament makes plain the type and its fulfilment and leaves the 'argument' from the fulfilment of the Scriptures more convincing today than when it was stated in terms of the inspiration of written records, whether by Liddon or by Sanday. Events are fulfilled in events; there is a 'real correspondence' in the things which happened, not merely in the minds of the interpreters; the Old Testament *Heilsgeschichte* discloses a plan of the divine action which the *kerygma* of the New Testament declares to have been triumphantly carried out. It is a plan which is fulfilled in a pattern of birth, baptism, temptation, failure, death and resurrection.

the student has been wearied by J, E, D, P and the rest, and he has never come to see why such studies—or indeed the Old Testament itself—are important for any other purpose than that of passing examinations in the biblical literature.

The Old Testament history begins with the mystery of the adoption by God of those Hebrews who were enslaved in Egypt; and thus Israel, while still a helpless infant, became God's 'son' (Ex. 4.22f.) and at the same time became a nation (Deut. 26.5). 'When Israel was a child, then I loved him, and called my son out of Egypt' (Hos. 11.1). The infant Israel then passed through the baptism of death and resurrection in the Red Sea, where the hostile powers of evil were decisively defeated (Isa. 51.9f.). This mighty act of God defines the meaning of Baptism in the Bible and in the Church; it represents deliverance, but deliverance through death and resurrection. Professor Wingren states the matter succinctly: 'God's actions by which Israel becomes Israel are actions purifying all that goes by the name of man. Now among these divine actions of election there is one which is in a class by itself, the Exodus from Egypt through the Red Sea. There God's people received their baptism; there they were born, and there began their history (Ex. 13-15). "Our fathers were all under the cloud, and all passed through the sea, and all were baptized into Moses in the cloud and in the sea" (I Cor. 10.1f.). But it belonged to Israel's task that Israel as a people should be crushed. Only when, as a corn of wheat, it falls into the ground and dies, can it bear fruit. Only when it loses its power and glory and becomes the Suffering Servant of Yahweh can it spread abroad in the world and become a light to the nations (Isa. 53). That event, the event of death and resurrection, can be hinted at and foreshadowed in the old Covenant but it cannot *take place* till the old departs and the new arrives. When that has taken place, the new Covenant will have arrived. In Jesus' death and resurrection this took place; therefore that happened which is "baptism", "the crossing over", "the passing through", the forward march, transit through the swelling waters, through death and hell, and so the stepping ashore upon the strand of the new age, while the enemy is drowned in the depths.'[1] To be baptized means to die and rise again; therefore Jesus was baptized in the waters of Jordan in anticipation of the Exodus which he should accomplish by his death and resurrection in Jerusalem (Luke 9.36; 12.50); so Christians are baptized that they too may enter through death and resurrection into the new life of the Age to Come (Mark 10.38f.; Rom. 6.3-11). The theology of the Bible is a baptismal theology, and the 'type' of all baptism is God's mighty act in the deliverance of his infant 'son' at the Red Sea waters. Baptism is something which God does, not which men do; God's action precedes our faith and creates it. Israel's faith was response to God's action at the Baptism in the Sea. The confessions of Israel in the Old Testament are, as we have noted, kerygmatic in character; they are acknowledgments of what God has done, and therefore will do, for his people.

When Israel in the Wilderness of Sinai came to understand what God had done, the solemn act of 'confirmation' was made: Israel entered into Covenant with God, ratified in the blood of sacrifice, and made the 'confirmation' vow: 'All that Yahweh hath spoken we will do, and be obedient' (Ex. 24.7f.).[2] Tested in the Wilderness, but sustained by the Bread from Heaven, Israel went forth towards the Promised Land to fulfil the vocation of the priest-nation (Ex. 19.4-6), to bring the knowledge of God and of his salvation to all the

---

[1]   Gustaf Wingren, *The Living Word*, Eng. trans. by Victor C. Pogue (London, 1960) of *Predikan* (Lund, 1949), 150.

[2]   Whatever may be made necessary by the exigencies of a particular missionary or pastoral situation in which the Church finds herself in any given age, infant baptism remains the norm of Christian baptism because in the Bible faith is the response to what God *has done* for us, not the condition upon which he *will do* something for us; but faith must be personally confessed and the obligations implicit in baptism must be voluntarily undertaken at 'years of discretion', as Israel undertook the vow of obedience at Sinai. See further: Alan Richardson, *Introduction to the Theology of the New Testament*, 358-63.

nations. Such a vocation involved the self-sacrifice and death of the Servant-Nation, and Israel refused this costly obedience. Nevertheless Israel died; the very existence of the nation came to an end in 587 B.C., and God's 'son' was buried in the Exile in Babylon. Humanly speaking, that was the end of the story; the death foreshadowed in Israel's baptism had taken place, but it had not happened according to the divine intention, that is, as an expiation and an offering by God's 'son' for the sins of the world; it had happened, in spite of the divine intention, by reason of the disobedience of God's 'son', who had refused the appointed office of Servant. The tragedy was not that Israel had died, but that Israel had deserved to die (cf. Isa. 5). Nothing but a divine miracle could restore the lifeless corpse. Nevertheless, the prophets of the Exilic period, trusting not in Israel's merits but in the faithfulness of God, prophesied that the miracle would take place. The Deutero-Isaiah expected a new miracle of creation and redemption, comparable to that of the Exodus from Egypt (Isa. 43.1-7, 16f.). Jeremiah looked forward to the making of a New Covenant between God and a re-created people (Jer. 31.31-34). Ezekiel predicted the resurrection of the dead and scattered bones of Israel (Ezek. 37), a resurrection which would be a veritable re-creation of mankind through the inbreathed Spirit of God (37.14; cf. Gen. 2.7). The miracle indeed happened; Israel was redeemed from the death of the Exile and restored to the land which the Lord had promised to the fathers. But the prophets do not make the mistake of supposing that the restoration of Jerusalem and the Temple is the fulfilment of the divine plan in its completeness; the restored nation of Zerubbabel and Joshua, of Ezra and Nehemiah, is still a sinful nation, is still incapable of fulfilling the divine destiny of the Servant-Son, the light of the Gentiles and Saviour of the world. The restoration is only a 'type' of that eschatological salvation which God himself would bring; it is not the realization of the divine intention, but only the sign and promise of it (cf. Isa. 62); the new creation is at hand, but is not yet (Isa. 65.17, etc.). The history of Israel points forward to the advent of the salvation which it foreshadows but does not contain. It tells the story of Israel's birth as God's 'son'; Israel's baptism of death and resurrection; Israel's vow of obedience, made and broken; Israel's death and burial; and Israel's resurrection from the dead. But it tells the story in such a way as to indicate that these historical episodes are only the foreshadowing of the salvation that is to be accomplished in the Day of Yahweh.[1]

It is hardly surprising that the New Testament writers should have presented the significance of the person and work of Christ in categories drawn, not from Hellenistic religion, but from the Scriptures of the Old Testament: Christ had performed the task which Israel had failed to fulfil, the mission of the 'son' and 'servant' of God, through whose vicarious self-sacrifice the salvation of the world would be realised. Christ was the new Israel, the obedient Son and Suffering Servant of God, who by his self-oblation fulfilled in his own person the mission of the people of God. Unlike Israel, he *chose* to be baptized, thereby voluntarily accepting the way of obedience and death. Tempted, as Israel had been, in the Wilderness, he refused to put God to the test and overcame the Tempter. His New Law, given on the Mount, was perfectly kept by him alone, and the consequence of his obedience was his death upon the cross. Out of the apparently total failure of his mission came victory and life, the miracle of the resurrection, which involved nothing less than the resurrection of a new Israel in him, and not only a new Israel but a new Adam, the creation of a new

---

[1]   The prophetic history of Israel, thus very briefly and inadequately recapitulated here, is presented with deep insight and wide scholarship in G. A. F. Knight, *A Christian Theology of the Old Testament*, 202-17, to which the present writer acknowledges his debt.

humanity in his risen body, the Church of the Messiah. Israel's historical destiny had been fulfilled in Christ. The New Testament is the republication of the *kerygma* of the Old Testament in its fulfilled and finished form.

Regarded in this light, which is the light of the apostolic teaching itself, the view that the Jesus of history is hidden from our sight behind the *kerygma* of the early Church becomes untenable. The historical words of Jesus and the events of his life are not invented by the primitive Christian community to illustrate the Church's preaching (*Gemeinde-theologie*); on the contrary, they are recorded because they fulfil the *kerygma* of the Old Testament. There would have been no apostolic *kerygma* and no New Testament theology if the historical Jesus had not himself taught and demonstrated in his life that the promises of the Scriptures, the meaning of Israel's history, were fulfilled in his own words and deeds. The record of his words and deeds, as it has reached us in the canonical Gospels, is, of course, an historical record, and is therefore the legitimate subject of the techniques of modern historical criticism; but that same criticism, so far from leading to scepticism concerning the historicity of the figure of Jesus in the Gospels, will help us to 'trace the course of all things accurately from the first' and thus to 'know the certainty concerning the things in which we have been instructed' by the Evangelists themselves (cf. Luke 1.3f.). It will do this, however, only if by its means we understand the apostolic *kerygma,* as the Evangelists themselves understood it, in the light of the Old Testament Scriptures, for according to the New Testament it is *those* Scriptures, and only those, which are able to make us 'wise unto salvation through faith which is in Jesus Christ' (II Tim. 3.15). The New Testament has no meaning apart from the Old Testament, as the Church asserted by condemning Marcion. The historical reality of the Jesus of the Gospels vanishes in a cloud of Hellenistic speculation and becomes an incredible, spectral Gnostic heavenly man, if we have not learned from the Old Testament the pattern of the divine action amongst men (cf. Mark 12.24). By revealing to us that pattern, the modern critical and scientific study of the Bible as a whole can shew us that the Jesus of the Gospels is indeed the Jesus of *history,* of the real, substantial history of the people of God, 'part of the history of the world'. The Scriptures of the Old Testament attest the Jesus of *history* (cf. John 5.39); they assure us that he is real, that the apostolic testimony concerning him is true, because it proclaims a fulfilment which is necessarily involved in the pattern of the dealings of God with his people in their history. This is the meaning of the fulfilment of the Scriptures, as the New Testament itself understands the matter; this was the meaning of the Bible as a book of two Testaments to those who, under the inspiration of the Holy Spirit, drew up the canon of the Christian Scriptures; and this is the truth of the Bible in all the Christian centuries, including the age of science.

INDEX OF NAMES

Acton, J.E.E.D.A., Baron, 59 n.
Addison, Joseph, 20 n.
Albert, Prince Consort, 48
Albertus Magnus, 11
Alembert, J. le R. d', 33 n., 39
Alkarismi, 16 n.
Althaus, Paul, 106 n., 112 n., 117 n.
Anne, Queen, 19
Aquinas, St Thomas, 11, 22, 38, 70
Archimedes, 15
Aristotle, 10–4, 24, 43, 55
Arnold, Matthew, 45 n., 61, 65 n., 73
Arnold, Thomas, 58 f.
Augustine, St, 10, 74, 104
Aurelius, Marcus, 46, 74
Averroes, 11

Bacon, Francis, Baron Verulam, 19
Baillie, Donald M., 148
Baillie, John, 27 n., 92 n., 121 n., 162
Barberini, Cardinal (Urban VIII), 17 n.
Barnes, E. W., 65
Barth, Karl, 57, 63, 78, 87–101, 113 n., 117, 119 f., 124–6
Bartsch, H. W., 106 n.
Beck, J. T. von, 122
Beerbohm, Max, 45 n.
Bernard, St, 104
Bloch, M., 126
Bornkamm, Günther, 144 n.
Bossuet, J. B., 44, 51 n., 56
Boyle, Robert, 23, 32
Brahe, Tycho, 13, 21
Braithwaite, R. B., 147 n.
Bretschneider, K. G., 97 n.
Bright, John, 77 n.
Brunner, Emil, 77, 89 n., 92 n., 149 n.
Buber, Martin, 102
Bull, George, 51 n.
Bultmann, Rudolf, 101, 104–19, 123, 130 n., 133 f., 143 f., 146, 157
Bulwer, E. (Lord Lytton), 45
Burgon, J. W., 60, 67
Buri, Fritz, 123 n.

Burnet, Gilbert, 44
Butler, Joseph, 20, 35, 36 n., 38
Butterfield, Herbert, 22 n., 24 n., 34 n.

Calvin, Jean, 70
Carlyle, Thomas, 46
Caspar, Max, 22 n.
Cavendish, Henry, 32
Celeste, Sister Maria, 18 n.
Chadwick, Henry, 39 n.
Chadwick, W. Owen, 51 n.
Chambers, Robert, 48
Charles II, King, 19
Church, R. W., 49, 60, 65
Clagett, Marshall, 13 n.
Clarendon, Edward Hyde, Earl of, 44, 72
Clarke, Samuel, 36 n., 37 n.
Cockshut, A. O. J., 102 n.
Colenso, J. W., 61
Coleridge, S. T., 39 f., 56 f.
Collingwood, R. G., 146 n.
Confucius, 74
Constantine, 18, 39, 43
Copernicus, 9 f., 16, 21
Creed, J. M., 87 n.
Creighton, Mandell, 59
Crombie, A. C., 24 n.
Cromwell, Oliver, 41
Cullmann, Oscar, 122 n., 132–7, 139 f., 176 n.

Dante, 10
d'Alembert, J. le R., 33 n., 39
Darwin, Charles, 36 n., 48 f., 69
Democritus, 33
Descartes, René, 22
d'Holbach, P. H. D., Baron, 33
Dickinson, Lowes, 135 n.
Diderot, Denis, 33 n.
Diem, Hermann, 103 n., 125 n.
Dodd, C. H., 112 n., 128–31
Döllinger, J. J. I. von, 59 n.
Drake, Stillman, 17 n.
Drews, Arthur, 142 n.
Dryden, John, 40 n.

Einstein, Albert, 17 n.
Eliot, George, 50 n.
Epicurus, 150
Euclid, 14

Farrar, F. W., 65 n.
Farrer, A. M., 77 n., 158–63
Feuerbach, L. A., 117
Finley, M. I., 42 n.
Fontenelle, B. le B. de, 34
Forsyth, P. T., 97
Foster, M. B. 27
Frankfurt, H., 150 n.
Frederick the Great, 78
Freeman, E. A., 59
Friedman, S., 102 n.
Froude, J. A., 59 n., 61

Galileo, Galilei, 10 n., 16–8, 24 f.,
  27–9
Gardner, Helen, 161 n.
Garvie, A. E., 86 n.
George II, King, 58
Gibbon, Edward, 43 f., 45, 56
Glass, Bentley, 48 n.
Gogarten, F., 89 n.
Gore, Charles, 66, 73
Gray, Asa, 60
Green, John Richard, 45, 59 n.
Guthrie, Shirley C., Jr., 122 n.

Hall, C. A. M., 122 n.
Hanson, R. P. C., 75 n., 178 n.
Harnack, Adolf von, 85, 87–9, 107,
  124
Hart, H. St. J., 57 n.
Headlam, A. C., 67 n.
Hegel, G. W. F., 47 f., 84–6, 88
Heidegger, Martin, 101–3
Herder, J. G., 88
Herodotus, 44, 54
Herrmann, W., 85, 113 n.
Hesse, Mary B., 146 n.
Hobbes, Thomas, 31 n.
Hocking, W. E., 90 n.
Hofmann, J. J. C. von, 122
Holbach, P. H. D. von, Baron, 33
Hollinshed, 44
Hood, Thomas, 165
Hort, F. J. A., 63–5, 97
Horton, Walter M., 91 n.
Hoskyns, Sir Edwyn C., 88 n.

Hume, David, 33, 45
Huxley, T. H., 47, 49

Inge, W. R., 65

James, D. G., 31 n.
Jaspers, Karl, 103
Jowett, Benjamin, 61, 65
Julian the Apostate, 18
Justin Martyr, 75

Kaftan, J. W. M., 85
Kattenbusch, F., 85
Keble, John, 66
Kepler, Johannes, 21 f., 28 n.
Knight, G. A. F., 72 n., 179, 184 n.
Kierkegaard, Søren, 50–2, 90, 103,
  107 n., 116

Lampe, G. W. H., 178
Laplace, P. S., 28 n., 132
Lavoisier, Antoine, 32
Leaney, A. R. C., 30 n.
Leavis, F. R., 39 n., 57 n.
Leibnitz, G. W., 36 n.
Lessing, G. E., 39, 51 n., 135
Lewis, C. S., 74
Lewis, H. D., 74 n.
Lichtenberger, F., 79 n., 97 n.
Liddon, H. P., 60, 66 f., 71 f., 172 n.,
  180
Lightfoot, John, 42 n.
Lightfoot, J. B., 63, 65, 97
Linnaeus, C., 32
Lippershey, H., 25
Livy, 44
Locke, John, 37
Lombard, Peter, 70
Loisy, Alfred F., 87 n.
Loofs, F., 85
Lovell, A. C. B., 29 n., 102
Lucretius, 33
Luther, Martin, 21, 74, 86, 104, 118
Lyman, Eugene W., 90 n.
Lytton, Lord, 45

Mabillon, J., 43, 56
Macaulay, Rose, 21 n.
Macaulay, T. B., Lord, 46 f., 72
Macintosh, D. C., 90 n.
Mackintosh, H. R., 77, 82 n., 86 n.
Macquarrie, John, 101 n.

Malevez, L., 120 n.
Marcion, 185
Marx, Karl, 47 f.
Mascall, E. L., 27 n., 154 n.
Melanchthon, 21
Milik, J. T., 30 n.
Mill, J. S., 39, 57
Montfaucon, B., 43
Morgan, G. Campbell, 94 n.
Mortimer, Ernest, 22 n.
Moule, H. C. G., 94 n.
Mozley, J. B., 38
Mozley, J. K., 86 n.
Muggeridge, Malcolm, 49 n.
Muratori, L. A., 43

Newman, J. H., Cardinal, 50 f., 59
Newton, Sir Isaac, 19, 23, 28, 32, 41, 49, 132, 165
Nielsen, E., 77 n.
Nineham, D. E., 77 n., 130 n.

Oman, John, 83 n.
Orr, James, 94 n.
Osiander, 21

Paley, William, 36, 49
Pascal, Blaise, 22, 102, 104, 121, 165
Pattison, Mark, 61, 77
Paulus, H. E. G., 79
Pearson, Hesketh, 49 n.
Pearson, John, 70
Petavius, D. (Petau), 51 n.
Pilkington, Roger, 23 n.
Plato, 14, 55, 74, 83, 150
Plutarch, 44, 143
Polanyi, Michael, 104 n.
Pope, Alexander, 33 n.
Priestley, J. B., 170
Priestley, Joseph, 32
Ptolemy of Alexandria, 10, 12
Pusey, E. B., 59–61, 65 f., 67, 80 n.
Pythagoras, 14

Rad, Gerhard von, 173 f.
Ramsey, Ian T., 153 n.
Ranke, Leopold von, 49
Raven, Charles E., 23 n.
Ray, John, 23, 32, 36 n.
Richardson Alan, 38 n., 54 n., 75 n., 92 n., 104 n., 108 n., 121 n., 144 n., 155 n., 160 n., 182 n.

Ritschl, Albrecht, 85 f., 112 n.
Roberts, T. A., 126 n., 135 n.
Robinson, James M., 125 n., 126 n., 130 n.
Rose, Hugh James, 80 n., 97 n.
Rousseau, J–J., 33, 40

Sancroft, William, 36
Sanday, William, 67–76, 180
Santillana, G. de, 17 n.
Schlegel, Friedrich von, 79, 83
Schleiermacher, F. D. E., 56 f., 63, 78–91, 113 n.
Schweitzer, Albert, 123
Scott, Sir Walter, 45
Seeley, Sir John, 65 n.
Selwyn, E. Gordon, 66
Shaftesbury, Lord (Anthony Ashley Cooper), 61
Shakespeare, William, 10, 44
Sherlock, Thomas, 37 n.
Smith, B. A., 64 n.
Smith, Ronald Gregor, 102 n.
South, Robert, 43
Spencer, Herbert, 47
Stanley, A. P., 60 f., 65
Storr, Vernon F., 73
Strauss, David Friedrich, 50 f., 53, 64, 107 n.
Swinburne, A. C., 18 n.

Taylor, A. E., 10 n.
Temple, F., 61
Temple, W., 74, 159 n., 160 f.
Tennyson, Alfred, Lord, 69 n., 72, 102 n.
Thirlwall, Connop, 80 n.
Thomas, St, see Aquinas.
Thomas à Kempis, 74
Thucydides, 44
Thurneysen, E., 89 n.
Tillemont, J., 43
Tillich, Paul, 155 f.
Toland, John, 37
Toynbee, Sir Arnold, 26
Troeltsch, Ernst, 85
Tycho Brahe, 13, 21

Unnik, W. C. van, 30 n.
Urban VIII, Pope, 17 n.
Ussher, James, 41 f.

Vidler, A. R., 87 n.
Voltaire, 39, 43 f.

Wallace, Alfred Russel, 48
Warfield, B. B., 94 n.
Werner, Martin, 123 n.
Wesley, John, 74
Westcott, B. F., 62 n., 63–5, 97, 132, 141
Whitehead, A. N., 26
Wieman, H. N., 91 n.
Wilberforce, Samuel, 49, 60
Wilhelm II, Kaiser, 88 f.
Williams, R., 60

Wilson, H. B., 60
Wilson, John, 154 n.
Wingren, Gustaf, 93 n., 181 f.
Winstanley, D. A., 62 n.
Wood, H. G., 142 n.
Woods, G. F., 154 n.
Woodward, E. L., 58 n.
Woollcombe, K. J., 178 n.
Wordsworth, William, 56
Wright, G. Ernest, 136–40 149 n., 173, 177 n.

Xenophanes, 150
Xenophon, 44

INDEX OF SUBJECTS

Absurd, The, 52
Alexandrian theology, 75 f.
Algebra, 16 n.
Allegorical interpretation, 178, 180
Almagest, 10
Anglo-Catholics, 65 f.
Angst, Anxiety, 103, 119, 156, 164
Anthropology, 92, 93 n., 98, 117–21, 163
Apostles' Creed, 109, 141, 143, 176
Arabian philosophy, 10 f.
Archetypal Humanity, 82 f.
Argument from Design, 19, 36, 48
Arithmetic, 15 f.
Aristotelian philosophy, 10–9, 24
Authentic existence, 103, 110 f., 119 f.
Authority of the Bible, 75, 94, 98, 165–7

Baptism, 181 f.
Bern School, 123 n.
Biblical Criticism, 50, 59 ff., 69, 77–80, 84 f., 94 f., 97 f., 185 f.

Catholicism (2nd Century), 84 f., 107 f.
Certitude, 116
Chalcedonian theology, 86 f., 108, 123 n.
Christ-myth theory, 142 n.

Christology, 81 f., 87, 91, 132–4
Chronology, 41 f., 165
Civilization, Christian, 24–6
Consciousness, religious; see Experience
Consistent eschatology, 123
Contemporaneity, 53
Conversion, 168
Cosmology, 9–31, 164–7
Covenant, 181–3
Creation, 27, 36 f., 139
Creeds, 173–6
Critical history, 54, 59–64
Criticism; see Biblical Criticism.

Death, 102 f., 167
Deism, 36–8, 81
Demythologizing, 108 f., 138 f., 143, 146
Design, 19, 36
Dialectical theology, 77, 89 f., 100
Dixie Professorship, 59
Docetism, 95 f., 105 f., 140
Dogma, Dogmatics, 82 f., 86, 91 139 f.

Ebionitism, 96
Ecclesiastes, 164
Empirical theology, 90 n.
Encyclopaedists, 33
English Historical Review, 59

Essays and Reviews, 58, 60 f.
Essays Catholic and Critical, 66
Eucharist, 171, 175
Evolution, 48 f., 69
Exile, The, 157, 183
Existentialism, 52, 90, 100–4, 153, 167
Existentialist theology, 100–21, 123
Exodus, The, 157, 172–5, 179, 181–3
Experience, religious, 56, 68–70, 74 f., 81–6, 88, 90 n., 91, 123
Experimental method, 9, 101

Form-criticism, 105, 123 f., 143
Fulfilment, 171 f.
Fundamentalism, 94

Gemeindetheologie, 105, 124, 143, 185
Geometry, 14
Gnostic mythology, 107–9, 134, 142 n., 186
God, 149–51
Gothic revival, 45
Graf-Wellhausen hypothesis, 77
Greek science, 14–6; history, 42–4, 54 f.
Greek (language), 152

Hebrew (language), 149, 152
Heilsgeschichte, meaning of, 122
Heilsgeschichte theology, 126–41, 174, 180
Hellenization, 87, 133 f.
Historical religion, 138, 157, 168–77
Historical theology, 61 f., 126
Historiography, Liberal, 125–8, 130, 132
History, nature of, 145–7
Holy Spirit; see Spirit

Images, poetic, 145–63, 172
Imagination, 145, 158–63
Inductive theology, 70–2
Inerrancy of Scripture, 67–70, 94 n., 161 f., 166
Infant baptism, 182 n.
Inquisition, 16, 17 n., 29
Inspiration of Scripture, 67–76, 86, 95 f., 160–2, 172 n., 177

'Jesus of history' research, 86, 96, 98 f., 105, 123–5, 130, 185

Job, Book of, 28 f.
Judgments of Value, 85, 112 n., 123

Kerygma, 105–14, 127–9, 154, 157, 173–6, 185
Kingdom of God, 82, 86, 92

Lamentabili Decree, 51 n.
Latitudinarianism, 66
Liberal Evangelicals, 73
Liberal Catholicism, Liberal orthodoxy, 65 f., 68
Liberal Protestantism, 39 n., 65, 67 n., 84–9, 97 f., 105–7, 112, 125
Liberal theology, 64–6
Liberal thought, 60–2, 73, 106
Linguistic analysis, 149, 153 f.
Logical Positivism, 85
Lux Mundi, 65 f.

Man; see Anthropology
Marxism, 15, 48, 142 n.
Materialism, 11, 33 f.
Mathematics, 14–6
Maurists, 55 f., 58
Metaphysics, rejection of, 85 f.
Method, scientific, 9–16, 28 n.; theological, 78
Miracles, 38, 81, 93, 95, 106, 109 112
Modernism, English, 65, 67 n.
Modernism, Roman Catholic, 51, 87 n.
Moravians, 78, 82
Mysticism, 86, 89 f.
Myth in the New Testament, 108 f., 133, 142 f., 155 n.
Mythology, 137 f., 142, 152 f.

Natural selection, 48 f.
Nature, The Religion of, 36 f.
Nature-religion, 138, 147, 174 f.
Nazis, 89
Nicene Creed, 176

Objective Knowledge, 101–4, 116, 125, 146
Old Testament, 136–9, 173–5, 185 f.
Ontological argument, 22
Origin of Species, 49, 58 n., 60

Paradox, 51–3

Passover, 171, 175
Philosophes, Les, 33, 34 n., 36, 39 f.
Platonic Christianity, 10
Positive historical religion, 81 f., 84, 91, 105
Positivism, 101, 125–8, 130–2, 153
Progress, 46 f.
Progressive revelation, 68 f., 74, 139
Ptolemaic system, 10–12
Pythagoreans, 10

Q, The document, 77
Qumran, 29, 134, 142

Rationalism, Rationalist theology, 36–9, 51, 78 f., 81, 83, 86, 126, 150 f.
Rationalist myth, 18
Reason, Age of, 31 n.
Reason, Religion of, 36 f., 81
Recital, Theology of, 137, 139, 173–6
Regius Professorships of History, 58 n.
Religion, 150
Religions, 81 f., 91, 156–8, 175
Religion of Jesus, 87, 107
Religion of Nature, 36 f.
Resurrection of Christ, 81, 110 f., 127 f., 130–2, 147 f., 173
Revelation, 29–31, 37 f., 62, 69 f., 80, 83 f., 91, 93–6, 115, 134 f., 141, 159–62
Ritschlianism, 85–8, 90 n., 112 f.
Romantic Movement, 56, 69, 73, 76, 78, 83, 88 f., 96

Royal Society, 19

Sceptical criticism, 50, 53, 79, 80 n., 105–7, 123 f., 144, 185
Scholasticism, 89, 96, 140, 160
Science, meanings of, 14
Scientific history, 54
Scientific knowledge, 101–4, 164–7
Spirit, Holy, 94–6, 159, 162, 168, 176, 186
St-Maur, Congregation of, 55 n., 58
Subjectivism, 99
Subjectivity, 52, 75, 90, 101–4, 115 f.
Symbolism, Symbols, 151–8
Systematic theology, 70

Teleological argument, 19, 36, 48
Theoria, 14, 116
Tractarians, 51, 59–61, 65
Tradition, 96
Trinity, 82
Tripos, Theological, 62
Tübingen, 21
Tübingen School, 50, 84 f.
Typology, 176–9

Value-judgments, 85, 112 n.
Verbal inspiration, 67, 94 n.
Verification, 101, 104

Waverley Novels, 45
Witches, 21 f., 68
Word of God, 94–6, 163
Worship, Early Christian, 175 f.